ADOBE® FIREWORKS® CS5
CLASSROOM IN A BOOK®

The official training workbook from Adobe Systems

Adobe

Adobe Press books are published by Peachpit, a division of Pearson Education located in Berkeley, California. For the latest on Adobe Press books, go to www.adobepress.com. To report errors, please send a note to errata@peachpit.com. For information on getting permission for reprints and excerpts, contact permissions@peachpit.com.

Printed and bound in the United States of America

ISBN-13:   978-0-321-70448-1
ISBN-10:   0-321-70448-7

9 8 7 6 5 4 3 2 1

WHAT'S ON THE DISC

Here is an overview of the contents of the Classroom in a Book disc

The *Adobe Fireworks CS5 Classroom in a Book* disc includes the lesson files that you'll need to complete the exercises in this book, as well as other content to help you learn more about Adobe Fireworks CS5 and use it with greater efficiency and ease. The diagram below represents the contents of the disc, which should help you locate the files you need.

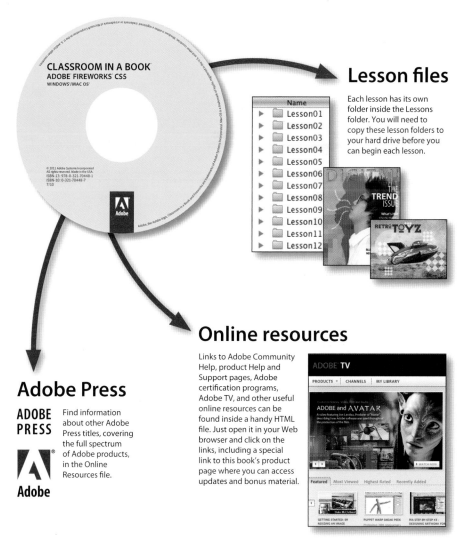

Lesson files

Each lesson has its own folder inside the Lessons folder. You will need to copy these lesson folders to your hard drive before you can begin each lesson.

Online resources

Links to Adobe Community Help, product Help and Support pages, Adobe certification programs, Adobe TV, and other useful online resources can be found inside a handy HTML file. Just open it in your Web browser and click on the links, including a special link to this book's product page where you can access updates and bonus material.

Adobe Press

Find information about other Adobe Press titles, covering the full spectrum of Adobe products, in the Online Resources file.

CONTENTS

BONUS SUPPLEMENTAL CHAPTERS 12 AND 13 ARE LOCATED ON THE COMPANION DISC

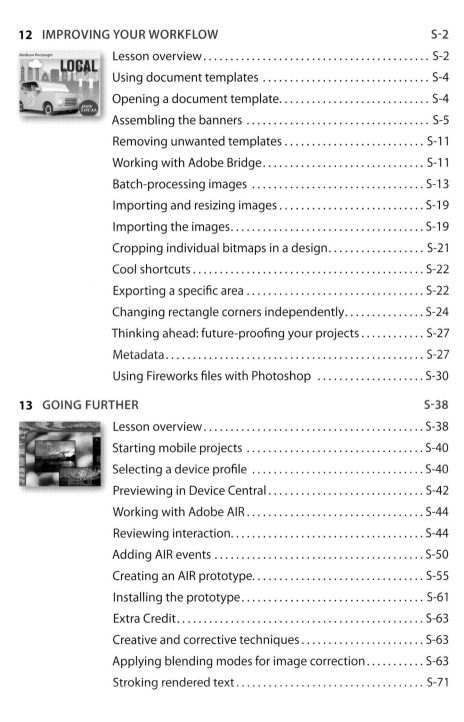

GETTING STARTED

Adobe Fireworks® is a professional imaging application that combines vector and bitmap imaging technologies and techniques in a single graphics application. This unique approach to imaging is due to the specific focus of Fireworks, which is creating and manipulating screen graphics for the Web or for other screen-based tools such as mobile applications or Adobe Flash® products. Fireworks is a tool that lets you quickly and easily create, edit, or alter graphics and designs. And it's a blast to work with, too!

With the release of Adobe Fireworks CS5, the program has gained even more distinction as a unique application for *rapid prototyping.* The built-in flexibility of Fireworks and its "everything is editable all the time" mandate have been present since it was created. When you're creating mockups and prototypes, where client or design changes can come fast and furious, this type of flexibility is very important. Features such as multiple pages, Device Central and Photoshop integration, and workflows like FXG 2.0 export and AIR prototyping make Fireworks an essential tool in the design process.

About Classroom in a Book

Adobe Fireworks CS5 Classroom in a Book is part of the official training series for Adobe graphics and publishing software developed by experts in association with Adobe Systems. The lessons are designed to let you learn at your own pace. If you're new to Adobe Fireworks, you'll learn the fundamental concepts and features you'll need in order to begin to master the program. And, if you've been using Adobe Fireworks for a while, you'll find that Classroom in a Book teaches advanced features, including tips and techniques for using the latest version of the application and for creating web and application prototypes. Although each lesson provides step-by-step instructions for creating a specific project, there's room for exploration and experimentation. You can follow the book from start to finish, or do only the lessons that match your interests and needs. Each lesson concludes with a review section summarizing what you've covered.

What's in this book

This edition covers many new features in Adobe Fireworks CS5, such as Adobe Device Central integration, the new Compound Shape tool, enhancements to the Properties panel, improved text handling, and exporting graphics for use in Flash Catalyst.

An overview of the new Adobe interface is covered in the first lesson, where you will learn how to configure the panels and document windows in Fireworks to suit your workflow. You will learn how to edit bitmap images and work with vector paths to create web interfaces. You will learn how to create and edit symbols, a powerful feature of Fireworks, and learn how Fireworks integrates with other Adobe CS5 applications like Dreamweaver, Photoshop, Bridge, and Flash.

Prerequisites

Before you begin to use *Adobe Fireworks CS5 Classroom in a Book*, you should have a working knowledge of your computer and its operating system. Make sure that you know how to use the mouse and standard menus and commands, and also how to open, save, and close files. If you need to review these techniques, see the documentation included with your Microsoft Windows or Macintosh system.

Installing Adobe Fireworks

Before you begin using *Adobe Fireworks CS5 Classroom in a Book,* make sure that your computer is set up correctly and that it meets the necessary system requirements for software and hardware. You'll need a copy of Adobe Fireworks CS5, of course, but it's not included with this book. If you haven't purchased a copy, you can download a 30-day trial version from www.adobe.com/downloads. For system requirements and complete instructions on installing the software, see the Adobe Fireworks CS5 Read Me file on the application DVD or on the Web at www.adobe.com/support.

Make sure that your serial number is accessible before installing the application.

Starting Adobe Fireworks

You start Fireworks just as you do most software applications.

To start Adobe Fireworks in Windows:

Choose Start > All Programs > Adobe Fireworks CS5.

To start Adobe Fireworks in Mac OS X:

Open the Applications/Adobe Fireworks CS5 folder, and then double-click the Adobe Fireworks CS5 application icon.

Copying the Classroom in a Book files

The *Adobe Fireworks CS5 Classroom in a Book* CD includes folders containing all the electronic files for the lessons in the book. Each lesson has its own folder; you must copy the folders to your hard disk to complete the lessons. To save room on your disk, you can install only the folder necessary for each lesson as you need it, and remove it when you're done.

To install the lesson files, do the following:

1 Insert the *Adobe Fireworks CS5 Classroom in a Book* CD into your CD-ROM drive.

2 Browse the contents and locate the Lessons folder.

3 Do one of the following:

- To copy all the lesson files, drag the Lessons folder from the CD onto your hard disk.

- To copy only individual lesson files, first create a new folder on your hard disk and name it **Lessons**. Then, open the Lessons folder on the CD and drag the lesson folder or folders that you want to copy from the CD into the Lessons folder on your hard disk.

Note: The CD also contains two bonus lessons and their accompanying lesson files. Chapter 12 discusses how to improve your Fireworks workflow and Chapter 13 discusses some of the more complex capabilities of Fireworks and integration between other Creative Suite software. PDFs of these two chapters are located in the Bonus Chapters folder on the disc, and their lesson files are located in the Lessons folder.

Additional resources

Adobe Fireworks CS5 Classroom in a Book is not meant to replace documentation that comes with the program or to be a comprehensive reference for every feature. Only the commands and options used in the lessons are explained in this book. For comprehensive information about program features and tutorials, refer to these resources:

Adobe Community Help: Community Help brings together active Adobe product users, Adobe product team members, authors, and experts to give you the most useful, relevant, and up-to-date information about Adobe products. Whether you're looking for a code sample or an answer to a problem, have a question about the software, or want to share a useful tip or recipe, you'll benefit from Community Help. Search results will show you content not only from Adobe but also from the community.

With Adobe Community Help you can:

- Access up-to-date definitive reference content online and offline
- Find the most relevant content contributed by experts from the Adobe community, on and off Adobe.com
- Comment on, rate, and contribute to content in the Adobe community
- Download Help content directly to your desktop for offline use
- Find related content with dynamic search and navigation tools

To access Community Help: If you have any Adobe CS5 product, you already have the Community Help application. To invoke Help, choose Help > Fireworks Help. This companion application lets you search and browse Adobe and community content, plus you can comment on and rate any article just like you would in the browser. However, you can also download Adobe Help and language reference content for use offline. You can also subscribe to new content updates (which can be automatically downloaded) so that you'll always have the most up-to-date content for your Adobe product at all times. You can download the application from www.adobe.com/support/chc/index.html.

Adobe content is updated based on community feedback and contributions. You can contribute in several ways: add comments to content or forums, including links to web content; publish your own content using Community Publishing; or contribute Cookbook Recipes. Find out how to contribute: www.adobe.com/community/publishing/download.html.

See http://community.adobe.com/help/profile/faq.html for answers to frequently asked questions about Community Help.

Adobe Fireworks Help and Support: See www.adobe.com/support/fireworks to find and browse Help and Support content on adobe.com.

Adobe TV: http://tv.adobe.com is an online video resource for expert instruction and inspiration about Adobe products, including a How To channel to get you started with your product.

Adobe Design Center: www.adobe.com/designcenter offers thoughtful articles on design and design issues, a gallery showcasing the work of top-notch designers, tutorials, and more.

Adobe Developer Connection: www.adobe.com/devnet is your source for technical articles, code samples, and how-to videos that cover Adobe developer products and technologies.

Resources for educators: www.adobe.com/education includes three free curriculums that use an integrated approach to teaching Adobe software and can be used to prepare for the Adobe Certified Associate exams.

Also check out these useful links:

Adobe Forums: http://forums.adobe.com lets you tap into peer-to-peer discussions, and questions and answers on Adobe products.

Adobe Marketplace & Exchange: www.adobe.com/cfusion/exchange is a central resource for finding tools, services, extensions, code samples, and more to supplement and extend your Adobe products.

Adobe Fireworks CS5 product home page: www.adobe.com/products/fireworks

Adobe Labs: http://labs.adobe.com gives you access to early builds of cutting-edge technology, as well as forums where you can interact with both the Adobe development teams building that technology and other like-minded members of the community.

Also check out these useful links:

- Community MX (www.communitymx.com) for additional free and commercial tutorials and samples

- Fireworks Zone—a tutorial, art, and news resource on all things Fireworks (www.fireworkszone.com)

- Fireworks Guru, the community forum where Fireworks enthusiasts share ideas, artwork, and solutions to design challenges (www.fireworksguruforum.com)

- Sarthak, the regularly updated Fireworks blog of Sarthak Singhal, a member of the Fireworks engineering team (blogs.adobe.com/sarthak)

- Adobe Fireworks Team blog, where you can learn the latest news from the people directly responsible for bringing you Adobe Fireworks (http://blogs.adobe.com/fireworks/)

- Johndunning.com, a prolific creator of Fireworks extensions, designed to make your job even easier (http://johndunning.com/fireworks/)

Adobe certification

The Adobe training and certification programs are designed to help Adobe customers improve and promote their product-proficiency skills. There are four levels of certification:

- Adobe Certified Associate (ACA)
- Adobe Certified Expert (ACE)
- Adobe Certified Instructor (ACI)
- Adobe Authorized Training Center (AATC)

The Adobe Certified Associate (ACA) credential certifies that individuals have the entry-level skills to plan, design, build, and maintain effective communications using different forms of digital media.

The Adobe Certified Expert program is a way for expert users to upgrade their credentials. You can use Adobe certification as a catalyst for getting a raise, finding a job, or promoting your expertise.

If you are an ACE-level instructor, the Adobe Certified Instructor program takes your skills to the next level and gives you access to a wide range of Adobe resources.

Adobe Authorized Training Centers offer instructor-led courses and training on Adobe products, employing only Adobe Certified Instructors. A directory of AATCs is available at http://partners.adobe.com.

For information on the Adobe Certified programs, visit www.adobe.com/support/certification/main.html.

1 GETTING TO KNOW THE WORKSPACE

Lesson overview

In this lesson, you will get up to speed on the Adobe Fireworks CS5 interface. You'll learn how to do the following:

- Set up a new document

- Open an existing document

- Draw a vector shape

- Get acquainted with the Tools panel

- Save a file

- Use the Properties panel to change attributes of a selected object

- Customize the workspace

- Work with multiple documents in Tab view

- Use the History panel

 This lesson takes approximately 90 minutes to complete. Copy the Lesson01 folder into the Lessons folder that you created on your hard drive for these projects (or create it now, if you haven't already done so). As you work on this lesson, you won't be preserving the start files; if you need to restore the start files, copy them from the *Adobe Fireworks CS5 Classroom in a Book* CD.

Fireworks shares a common interface with Adobe
Photoshop, Adobe Dreamweaver, Adobe Flash,
Adobe Illustrator, and Adobe InDesign. This common
user interface makes it easy to switch from one
application to another without feeling lost.

Getting started in Adobe Fireworks

Fireworks is a creative production tool, and sometimes with a creative tool, the hardest thing to do is decide where to start. We're here to help! Let's begin with a brand-new document and explore the interface in the process. As you work through this exercise, refer to the figure on page 5 to locate the main parts of the Fireworks interface.

1 Start Fireworks.

2 Choose Create New > Fireworks Document (PNG) from the Welcome screen. If you've previously changed your Preferences so that the Welcome screen does not show on startup, choose File > New.

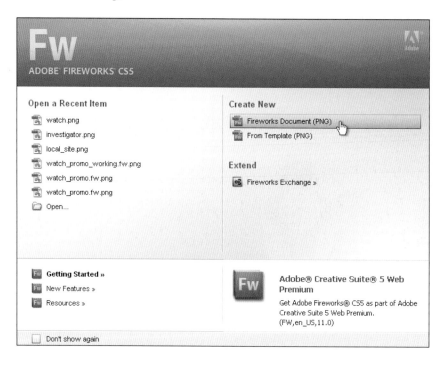

Note: New in Fireworks CS5 is the ability to create a new document from a template. Fireworks ships with several predesigned starter templates, and you can even create your own custom templates. You'll learn more about templates in Lesson 10.

The New Document dialog box is where you set the canvas size, color, and resolution for your new design.

3 Set both the width and the height of your document to 500 (pixels). Leave the resolution and canvas color at the default settings of 72 Pixels/Inch and White, and then click OK.

The New Document dialog box closes and a new blank document opens in the Fireworks work area, as shown in this screenshot of the Windows version of Fireworks.

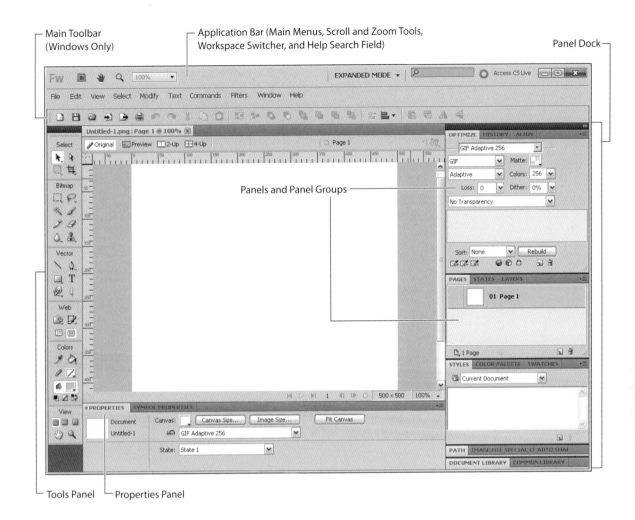

Main Toolbar (Windows Only)

Application Bar (Main Menus, Scroll and Zoom Tools, Workspace Switcher, and Help Search Field)

Panel Dock

Panels and Panel Groups

Tools Panel — Properties Panel

The default workspace in Fireworks for Windows consists of the Application bar and Main toolbar at the top of the screen, the Tools panel on the left, and open panels in the panel dock on the right. By default, when you have multiple documents open they appear as multiple tabs in one document window, but you can float individual documents by dragging their tabs away from the main Document window. The Fireworks user interface is similar to the ones used in Adobe Illustrator, Adobe Photoshop, and Adobe Flash, so learning how to use the tools and organize panels in one application means that you'll know how to use them in the others.

The initial workspace for the Mac version is similar, except the Application bar is separate from the Menu bar, and there is no Main toolbar. By default, the Mac interface is organized a little differently from the Windows interface. In Windows, all the panels and windows that belong to an application are contained within a rectangular frame that is distinct from other applications you may have open.

The area within the frame is opaque, completely obscuring any application windows that may be behind it.

It's possible to re-create this same behavior in the Mac version of Fireworks by turning on the Application Frame, which is disabled by default. To enable the Application Frame, choose Window > Use Application Frame (Control+Command+F). On a Mac, however, the Menu bar is always attached to the top of the screen and can't be moved, so it's not part of the Application Frame.

The default, on both Windows and Mac, is for multiple document windows to be opened in tabs. If you want to detach a document for side-by-side viewing, simply drag the tab away from the tab bar and it becomes its own document window. If you prefer individual document windows in the Mac version, you can disable tabs in the Preferences (choose Fireworks > Preferences and select the General category). You can dock numerous documents above and beside each other in what is called N-Up view. (To use N-Up view on the Mac, you must have the Application Frame enabled.)

Application Bar   Menu Bar   OS X Desktop

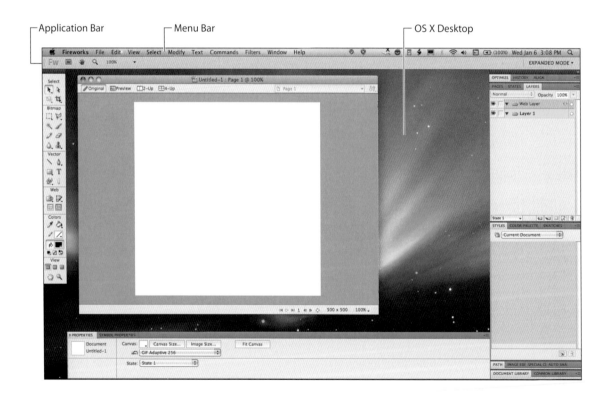

What is the right resolution?

Pixels per inch (ppi) is a unit of measure relative only to the print world. When dealing with screen graphics, your concern should be the *pixel dimensions* (640 x 480, 760 x 420, and so on). The default resolution Fireworks begins with is 96 ppi (72 ppi on a Mac), and it can be left as is. If you are planning to use Fireworks for a print project, ask your printer what resolution you should be using. A general guideline for print is 300 ppi. Be aware, however, that the strengths of Fireworks lie in screen graphics, not graphics intended for the printed page. For example, you cannot change the rulers to display inches—only pixels matter on the screen, so pixels are all you get for the rulers. Likewise, Fireworks does not understand or use CMYK color or printer profiles, so your end result may not print accurately.

On the plus side, Fireworks supports PDF export, so printing your designs, for example to show to a client, has become a bit more predictable.

Preparing the canvas

You should set (activate) a few features before you start working. These features will remain set from this point forward when you create or open a new document.

1   If the rulers are not visible, choose View > Rulers (Ctrl+Alt+R in Windows, Command+Option+R in Mac).

2   Choose View > Tooltips (Ctrl+] in Windows, Command+] in Mac).

Turning rulers on makes it much easier to align objects on your canvas; this is especially helpful when your work gets complex. Enabling tooltips provides you with extra information at the cursor position for the tool you're using.

Drawing a vector shape

Creating shapes will be an important part of any Fireworks project. The canvas is your working area for your designs. Objects that extend outside the canvas appear clipped, but the image information is not lost; just drag the object into the canvas (or resize the canvas) to show the full object.

1   Select the Rectangle tool from the Vector section of the Tools panel.

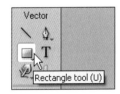

2   Click the Fill color box—the one with the small paint bucket to the left of it— in the Colors section of the Tools panel to set the fill color for the rectangle. The fill color is the one that will be inside your object.

3 Using the eyedropper pointer that appears, select black from the Fill Color pop-up window. Once the color is selected, the color selector closes automatically, and the color you chose is displayed in the color box.

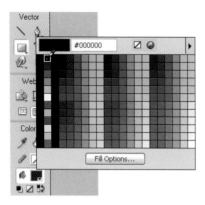

4 Bring the cursor to the upper-left corner of your canvas area. Note the small gray bubble, displaying *x* and *y* coordinates. This is the Tooltips feature at work, giving you the pixel-precise location of the cursor.

5 Position the cursor so both *x* and *y* read "0."

▶ **Tip:** Technically, you could accomplish everything you did here with the Rectangle tool by simply setting the canvas color of your new document to black. But using the shape gives you more flexibility as your project grows.

6 Hold down the mouse button, and drag to the bottom-right corner of the canvas. The tooltip follows the cursor.

7 Release the mouse button when you see the coordinates match your document dimensions of 500 x 500. The rectangle will stay selected after you release the mouse. (You can tell an object is selected by the light blue border around the object and the small control boxes at each corner.) The rectangle is a special, grouped vector object, so you won't see the blue border when it is selected (more on grouping objects in Lesson 2).

▶ **Tip:** If you didn't get an exact match for dimensions, you can tweak the vector shape's size in the Properties panel, located at the bottom of the interface. Click inside the Width or Height field and type the correct size. Tabbing, pressing Enter or Return, or clicking away from the field will lock any changes in place.

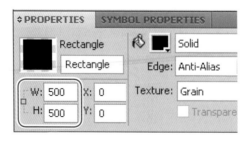

Saving the file

Before going any further, it's a good idea to save your work.

1 Choose File > Save As.

2 Browse to the Lesson01 folder.

3 Change the filename to **watch_promo.fw.png**.

4 From the Save As Type field, choose Fireworks PNG.

5 Click Save.

● **Note:** In Fireworks CS5, you can now lock the proportions of your objects from within the Properties panel by clicking on the small square to the left of the Width and Height fields. This makes it much easier to scale objects proportionately. If the small square linking the width and height is hollow, proportions are not constrained. Clicking on the square makes it solid and adds solid connecting lines between the Width and Height fields, locking the proportions of the selected object.

● **Note:** Since you began with a new, untitled document, you can also choose File > Save (Ctrl/Command+S) to display the Save As dialog box. Because you are using Fireworks image objects (the vector rectangle), Fireworks assumes you want the new design to remain as editable as possible, and gives you the option only of saving as a Fireworks PNG file (see the following screenshot). If you choose File > Save As, Fireworks gives you many more file format options to choose from.

More about the Fireworks PNG format

Like many applications, Fireworks has its own native format that gives you access to all the creative options within the program—in this case, a modified version of the PNG format. As you add effects, layers, or pages (to name a few features), this information is stored within the Fireworks PNG file so that you can open and edit the file easily at any time. However, this can cause a bit of confusion for new users, because there is also a standard, flattened PNG format common to many graphics applications. When you're saving files, Fireworks differentiates between these "flavors" by indicating "Fireworks PNG" or "Flattened PNG" in the Save As Type field.

From a user perspective, it can be helpful to add a moniker to the file name, as we have here by adding **.fw** to indicate this is a Fireworks PNG file. Adding a moniker makes it much easier to locate native Fireworks PNG files at a glance.

Using the Tools panel

The Tools panel in Fireworks is separated into six labeled areas: Select, Bitmap, Vector, Web, Colors, and View. This arrangement makes it easy for you to quickly identify the appropriate tool for the graphic object you plan to work on or create.

The Select tools let you select, crop, and even scale or distort objects. The main selection tool is the Pointer tool ( ).

The Bitmap tools are used for editing or creating new bitmap objects. You can make bitmap selections with any one of several bitmap selection tools, such as the Magic Wand or the Marquee tool. You can do basic photo editing by using the Rubber Stamp (also known as the Clone tool), or selectively sharpen, blur, lighten, darken, or smudge pixels that are part of a bitmap image. You can paint or draw bitmap objects using the Brush or Pencil tool. The only caveat is that Bitmap tools can't be used to alter vector objects.

The Vector tools let you create or edit vector paths and shapes. As you saw in the first exercise, you can draw vector shapes on the canvas quite easily. You can use the Pen tool to create your own custom shapes or paths. Of special note is the Text tool (T). Some people don't realize this, but text is actually a vector—be it in Photoshop, Microsoft Word, Fireworks, or many other applications. Vector tools can't be used to edit bitmap objects.

The Web toolset is not large, but it contains two important tools: the mainstays of Fireworks and its ability to create interactive documents and optimize graphics for use on the Web. You can create interactivity with the Hotspot tools, or take things further by creating interactive visual effects such as rollovers, using the Slice tool. The Slice tool also allows you to optimize specific graphic elements for the Web. The other two tools simply show or hide the web components on the canvas.

The Colors tools let you control Stroke and Fill colors. Remember, the roots of Fireworks are in the vector world, so you will not see Foreground and Background color options, as you would in primarily bitmap-editing software such as Photoshop. You can sample colors from anywhere on the desktop using the Eyedropper tool, or fill a bitmap selection with color by using the Paint Bucket or Gradient tool. You can also swap the fill and stroke colors or reset the fill and stroke to their defaults.

Last are the View tools. You can toggle between three views: Standard, Full Screen with Menus, and Full Screen (no menus or panels visible). The Zoom tool and Hand (scroll) tool are at the bottom of the View toolset. You can also toggle between views using the F key.

More tools than meet the eye

Take a closer look at the icons in the Tools panel. You will notice several that have a small triangle in the bottom-right corner. This triangle indicates that multiple tools are available from within that square. To access the other tools, click and hold the icon.

The three shapes at the top of this list are *vector primitives*, or basic shapes. Everything below the dividing line falls into the category of special vectors called Auto Shapes; they are controlled "under the hood" by JavaScript and are great for creating many common but complex vector shapes without the need of any drawing skills. You'll draw an ellipse in your document.

With the document we worked on previously open, do the following:

1   Make sure the rectangle on the canvas is deselected by clicking in the gray area outside the canvas. Then click and hold the Rectangle tool in the Vector tool area. A tool menu pops up.

2   Select the Ellipse tool.

3   In the Tools panel, set the Fill color to light gray from the color picker.

When you hold down the Rectangle tool icon, you see this list of all the common vector shapes Fireworks has to offer.

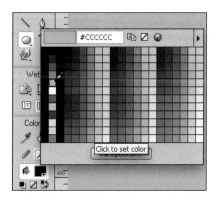

4   Move the cursor onto the canvas, and draw an oval (ellipse) that is 231 pixels wide by 401 pixels high.

5   Select the Pointer tool, and reposition the ellipse to an *x* and *y* value of 20 and 50, respectively.

6   Save the file.

What's a primitive shape?

The word *primitive* borrows the same definition used in many 3D modeling applications: *a geometric form or expression from which another is derived.* In other words, the Fireworks *Primitive* tools provide a start toward building shapes of your own.

Using the Properties panel

As you select different tools, the Properties panel updates and displays editable attributes for the selected tool. The Properties panel is context sensitive, so it changes based on the active selection on the canvas.

As we saw in the first exercise, it was easy to find and add a rectangle shape and change its fill color using the Tools panel. When a shape is selected, you can change many other vector attributes in the Properties panel.

1   Select the Pointer tool ( ) from the upper left of the Tools panel.

2   On the canvas, click on the black rectangle to select it.

3   In the Properties panel, choose Gradient > Linear from the Fill Category menu (next to the Fill Color box). The vector ellipse's fill color changes to a gradient.

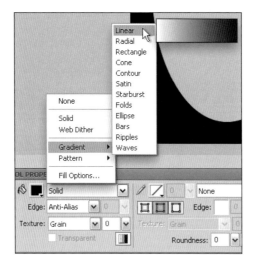

Next, you will set the colors for the gradient.

4   Click the Fill Color box to launch the Edit Gradient pop-up window. The top swatch sliders (little black boxes) control the opacity of the gradient. The swatches underneath the gradient allow you to change or add colors. You can ignore them for now, though, as we're going to keep this nice and simple.

5 Click the Preset combo box and select the White, Black preset.

The gradient fill now runs vertically, starting with white at the top and fading to black at the bottom.

6 When you're done, click away from the Edit Gradient pop-up window to close it.

Some gradient ranges produce a banding effect, which generally is not desirable. You can quickly dither a gradient to produce a higher-quality effect.

7 Click the Gradient Dither icon in the Properties panel.

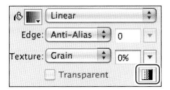

You will see a dramatic change to the quality of the gradient tonal range.

8 Save the file once again.

Configuring panels and panel groups

Your computer monitor is one of those places where you're always trying to *make more room*. No matter what size the screen is, we designers always want more room to build our designs. A fair portion of the interface is taken up by panels by default. Panels contain controls that help you edit aspects of a selected object or elements of a document. Each panel is draggable, so you can group panels in custom arrangements.

Many panels are visible by default in an area on the right side of the interface called the panel dock. A *dock* is a collection of panels or panel groups displayed together, usually in a vertical arrangement. Resizing the docked panels is one way to quickly make more room for your design.

Note: Try changing the gradient colors manually by clicking on the small color swatches. If you want to add other colors, just click the mouse somewhere along the gradient preview and choose a new color for the new swatch. Feel free to experiment with the other Fill categories, but remember to come back to the White, Black gradient preset before continuing with the lesson.

Note: In the Gradient Editor you can quickly reverse the gradient direction by clicking the Reverse Gradient button.

Tip: There are many cool—and free—command panels for Fireworks; these are generally referred to as extensions. One very nifty extension for Fireworks is the Gradient panel. To learn more about it, visit www.adobe.com/devnet/fireworks/articles/gradient_panel.html.

You can group and ungroup panels by dragging them into and out of the existing panel groups docked to the side of the screen.

By default, the dock is in Expanded Mode, in which the foremost panel in each group is fully expanded so you can see its features. Collapse individual panel groups by clicking once (or double-clicking on a Mac) on the empty area of the gray tab bar.

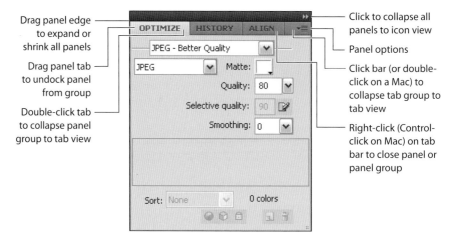

Drag panel edge to expand or shrink all panels

Drag panel tab to undock panel from group

Double-click tab to collapse panel group to tab view

Click to collapse all panels to icon view

Panel options

Click bar (or double-click on a Mac) to collapse tab group to tab view

Right-click (Control-click on Mac) on tab bar to close panel or panel group

In the Application bar you can see the current workspace configuration in the Workspace Switcher. You can quickly reduce the dock width by choosing a different workspace.

1   Select the Workspace Switcher and choose Iconic Mode. All panels collapse, and the dock narrows to display only panel icons.

2   Click any panel icon. The panel group expands, and the chosen panel becomes active.

3   Click the panel icon (or the double-arrow icon) to return the group to its collapsed state.

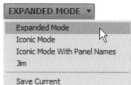

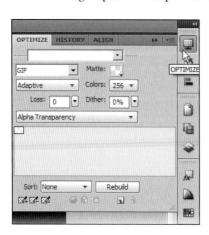

4 Position the mouse over different icons to see a tooltip that shows which panel each icon represents.

5 Choose Iconic Mode With Panel Names from the Workspace Switcher. This setting makes the docked panel groups wider, but not nearly as wide as the default Expanded Mode. If you want to free up desktop space but aren't sure of the tools icons, this mode might just be perfect for you.

▶ **Tip:** You can also quickly collapse the dock by double-clicking on the dark gray strip at the top of the dock.

Customizing panel arrangements

It's easy to arrange the panels and panel groups in a configuration that helps you work faster. For example, some designers like to be able to see both the Pages and Layers panels at the same time. In this exercise, you will separate the Pages panel from its current panel group.

1 Switch back to Expanded Mode.

2 Drag the Pages panel tab just above the panel group. A blue highlighted drop zone appears.

3 Release the mouse button; the Pages panel forms its own group, just above the Layers and States panel group.

● **Note:** You can access all the available panels in Fireworks by choosing the desired panel's name from the Window menu. In some cases, these panels will appear floating above the design.

4 Drag the States panel tab to the right of the Layers panel tab. Notice how easily they just slide across each other.

▶ **Tip:** You can also collapse the Properties panel by double-clicking on the empty area of the tab bar.

Creating custom workspaces

In addition to taking advantage of the existing preset workspaces, you can configure the workspace specifically to help you work the way that's best for *you*. You can also save these customized workspaces so that you can quickly switch from a compact mode to a dual-screen mode or even just a custom panel view that holds the panels you would use most often.

To create a custom workspace, set the panels you wish to see, at the desired size and visibility.

1 Select the Workspace Switcher.

2 Choose Save Current. A dialog box appears where you can name the new workspace arrangement.

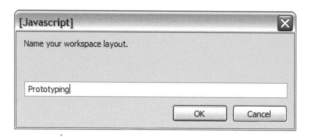

3 Name the workspace and click OK, or click Cancel if you don't want to save the configuration. If you save the workspace, it will appear in the Workspace Switcher from this point on.

Deleting a custom workspace

Although it's easy to *make* a custom workspace, it's not so easy to *delete* it. There is no way to remove a custom workspace within the Fireworks interface. You can overwrite the workspace by changing the panel setup and then saving the new workspace with the old name, but you're still stuck with the workspace.

To remove a custom workspace, you will need to go to Application Data\Adobe\ Fireworks CS5\Commands\Workspace Layouts in Windows or ~/Library/Application Support/Adobe/Fireworks CS5/Commands/Workspace Layouts/ (where "~" represents your Home folder) on the Mac. Then delete the JSP and XML files associated with your custom workspace.

Working with multiple documents

Before we finish this lesson, let's have a look at the Fireworks CS5 document window features. When you have more than one file opened, the document windows for each are tabbed and easily accessible.

1 Choose File > Open, and browse to the Lesson 1 Folder from the CD.

2 Ctrl-click (Windows) or Command-click (Mac) to select the watch.png and investigator.png files.

3 Click the Open button. If you haven't changed your Preferences from the defaults, all three files are now open in Fireworks and you can access each one by clicking on the appropriate tab at the top of the document window.

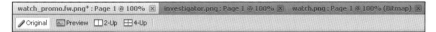

Creating a floating document window

Tabbed documents function much like the tabbed panels. You can drag them to change the tab order. You can even drag a tabbed document out from the tab bar to float it.

1 Click and hold on the watch.png tab, and drag it away from the other tabs. When you let go, it becomes a floating window.

Document-arrangement options don't stop there, however.

2 Drag the watch.png file to the right side of the main document window until you see a blue highlight (thin blue line) appear between the panel dock and the document window.

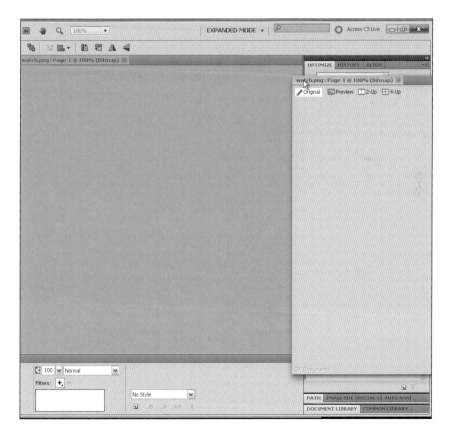

⬤ **Note:** If you have chosen not to use the Application Frame on the Macintosh (Window > Use Application Frame), your document windows will still open in tabs, but you won't be able to use the docked viewing mode described here. In the classic Mac view, you can either have documents tabbed together or floating, or a combination of both.

3 Release the window; you now have two sets of docked document windows. You can have as many files as you like docked in this manner.

Both floating and docked windows support tabbed documents.

4 Select the investigator.png file, and drag its tab over to the watch.png window.

5 Move the file so the cursor appears in the tab bar. You will see that familiar blue drop-zone indicator again. Release the file; it is now tabbed with the other document window.

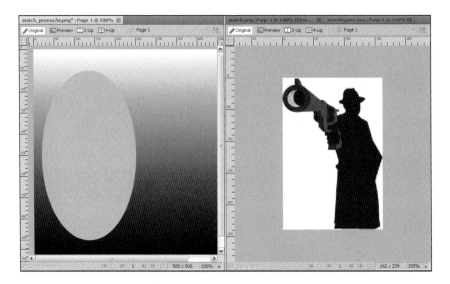

Dragging and dropping between floating windows

With the watch_promo.fw.png file now separate from the other two files, it's easy to drag and drop the watch and investigator images onto the canvas area of the promo file.

1 Select the Pointer tool (black arrow) from the upper left of the Tools panel.

2 Click to select the artwork in the investigator file, and drag it over to the promo design.

> **Tip:** Not only does Fireworks support layers and sublayers, just like Photoshop, but for even more control over your design structure, you can also have multiple objects in a single layer.

3 Position the image at the bottom of the design, near the right.

4 Release the mouse button.

The new image has been added to the current layer in the Layers panel.

5 Select the watch.png file, and use the Pointer tool to drag the watch from its own canvas to the promo canvas.

6 Position the Pointer tool near the left middle for now. The watch_promo.fw.png file should look something like the following figure. Adjust the positioning as necessary, and save the file.

● **Note:** Because Fireworks moves so seamlessly between vector and bitmap artwork, you probably didn't even realize that the investigator file was a vector object!

Undoing steps

The ability to reverse your actions is an all-important feature of imaging software. Fireworks gives you a couple of ways to undo an error. Undo is, of course, the tried-and-true, familiar method.

1 Press Ctrl+Z (Windows) or Command+Z (Mac). The last step you made is undone.

2 Press Ctrl+Z/Command+Z three more times. This takes you further back in the history of the document.

3 Press Ctrl+Y (Windows) or Command+Y (Mac). This reapplies the last undone step.

Another option exists: the History method.

4 Select the History panel from your grouped panels or choose Window > History. Make sure the watch_promo.fw.png file is selected.

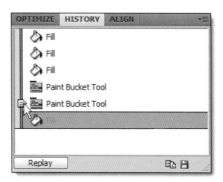

5 Drag the History slider (left of the panel) down until it can go no further.

6 Drag the slider up, and watch the promo canvas. As the slider reaches each previous step, you will see your documents change.

Creating custom commands with the History panel

Do you find yourself doing the same things over and over again in a file (or multiple files)? Save your history steps as a custom command, which you can then use again any time, from the Commands menu. This trick can eliminate some of your repetitive but necessary drudge work.

To save a custom command, simply select all the steps you need in the History panel, and then click the small floppy-disc icon in the lower-right corner of the panel. You will be prompted for a name. Make it short but relevant; it's the name that will appear in the Commands menu.

The History panel doesn't record mouse movements, so in order to get a complete custom command, use the keyboard commands and menu items.

Review questions

1 What is the importance of the Tools panel?

2 How do you collapse panels and why would you?

3 If you can't find a panel in the workspace, how can you locate it?

4 How does the Properties panel help when you are working on a design?

5 How do you access the hidden tools in the Tools panel?

Review answers

1 The Tools panel is where all the selection, editing, and creative tools are located. From cropping an image to scaling it, whether retouching or building vector objects or adding interactive elements, everything you need begins in the Tools panel.

2 You can collapse panels by choosing a different workspace, or by clicking on the dark gray bar at the top of a panel group. This can free up a significant amount of room in your workspace, letting you see more of your design without having to zoom out as much.

3 To open a panel, choose Window > [panel name], or press the panel's shortcut (listed in the Window menu).

4 The Properties panel is a context-sensitive panel, changing its options as you select different tools or various objects on the canvas. The Properties panel makes it easy to alter tool and object attributes from one handy location.

5 To display hidden tools, click and hold on a tool icon that has the small triangle in the bottom-right corner. A tool menu will pop up, displaying any tools hidden in that group.

2 THE PAGES, STATES, AND LAYERS PANELS: FUNDAMENTAL WORKFLOW TOOLS

Lesson overview

Layers are probably the most important workflow and design tool you have in Fireworks. Simply put, they add structure to your document. In this lesson, you'll learn how to do the following:

- Import new pages
- Create new layers
- Create sublayers
- Change the stacking order of layers
- Rename layers
- Protect layers and objects
- Access layer options
- Edit content on different states

 This lesson takes approximately 90 minutes to complete. Copy the Lesson02 folder into the Lessons folder that you created on your hard drive for these projects (or create it now, if you haven't already done so). As you work on this lesson, you won't preserve the start files. If you need to restore the start files, copy them from the *Adobe Fireworks CS5 Classroom in a Book* CD.

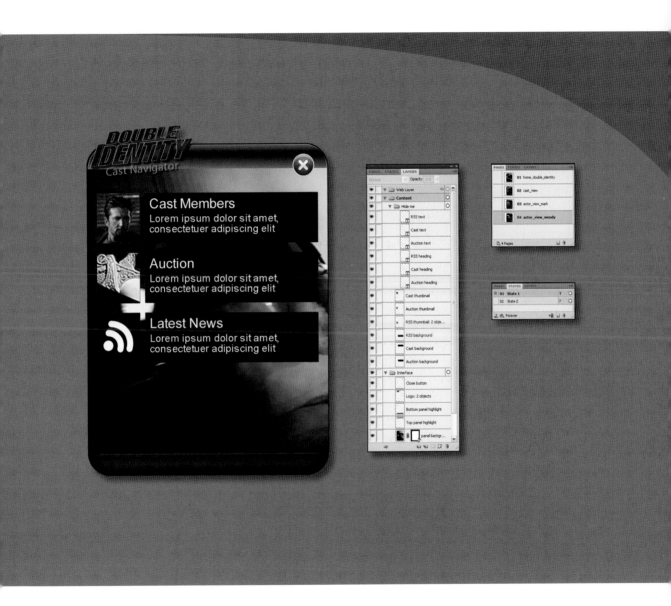

Understanding the relationship between pages, layers, and states is probably the most important concept to grasp in Fireworks. These elements add structure to your document.

About pages, layers, and states

A Fireworks document can contain multiple pages, layers, and states. At its simplest, a brand-new Fireworks document begins with a single page (Page 1), a single state (State 1), and two layers (the Web layer and Layer 1).

Pages

The ability to add multiple pages to a document means you can create and store multiple designs of different dimensions and resolution inside a single Fireworks file.

This improves asset management, because unique designs for one project can all be stored in the same file. Therefore, you can mock up an entire website or application design within a single file. Pages can then be linked using hotspots or slices to create a truly interactive experience for testing and proof of concept.

Each page can hold multiple layers and states.

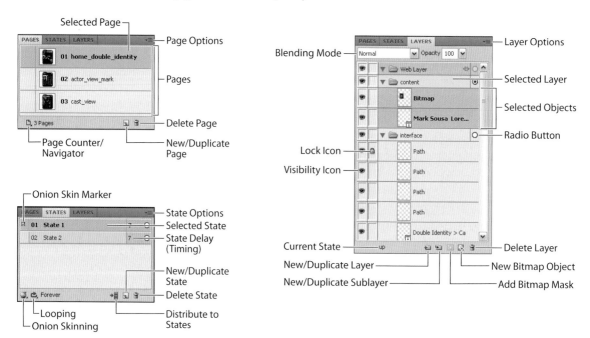

Layers

Layers help you organize and group your artwork, as well as specify which artwork is visible and how objects are stacked. Each layer can contain multiple bitmap, vector, and text objects.

With a simple design, you may be able to place all the objects in a single layer. But as you add more objects to a design, keeping everything in a single layer becomes problematic; it becomes harder to locate specific images or text areas because you have to scroll through a very long list.

Layers allow objects to be independent from one another. Used properly, they impose a sense of order in your document. You can add or remove layers, or the objects within them, without affecting other elements in the design. You can change how objects within layers interact with other layers by changing the stacking order of layers. As you change the order of layers, objects overlap differently. You can move objects from one layer to another as well.

You can hide layers from view, to make it easier to select or work with other objects, and you can lock layers so they will not be selected accidentally. You can even share layers across specific states or specific pages in a design.

States

States are used for three purposes:

- To create frame-by-frame animation.
- To show the different states of an object, such as the normal and hover states of a website navigation button.
- To control the visibility of objects based on user interaction. For example, hovering over a button displays a new button state, and then clicking that button displays new content elsewhere on the page.

Every page contains at least one state. A design requiring no interactivity may only need a single state. If interactivity or animation is required, new states are added. Each state can represent the visibility and position of objects on each layer.

Note: The interactivity described for states is controlled by adding special objects—slices and hotspots—to a special layer, called the Web layer. Regardless of your plans for the file, the Web layer cannot be deleted. To learn more about hotspots and slices, read Lessons 8 and 10.

Note: Web layers and regular layers can also contain sublayers that help you further organize your design. You will learn more about sublayers in this lesson.

Getting started

In this lesson, you'll be editing a mockup for an AIR application. You'll reorganize the file by working on the layers and add pages for the mockup created by another artist.

1   In Fireworks, choose File > Open and select the file cast_navigator.fw.png in the Lesson02 folder.

2   Click OK.

3   Select the Pages panel and, if necessary, drag the bottom of the Pages panel lower in the panel dock, so you can see all three pages.

4   Select the second page from the list. Notice how the design changes on the canvas. When you select a page, all you see on the canvas are the contents of that particular page.

You can change the order of pages in a document by dragging a page above or below another page.

5 Drag the page called actor_view_mark below the page named cast_view. This puts the pages in a more suitable order for your next task.

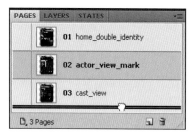

Importing pages

Next you will add pages to this mockup. Make sure the actor_mark_view page is still selected.

1 Choose File > Import, and open cast_navigator_assets.fw.png. The Import dialog box appears.

2 Choose Open, and the Import Page window appears. The document you're importing contains two pages, which you can preview by using the drop-down list at the top of the window or the navigation buttons below the preview image. You need to import the actor_view_wendy page first, so make sure that is the page currently displayed.

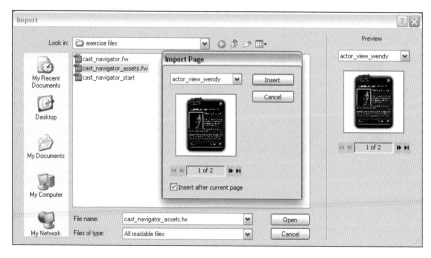

3 Select the Insert After Current Page option. This option creates a new page in your open file rather than importing the artwork onto the currently active page.

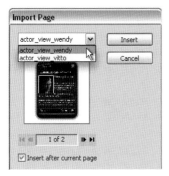

4 Click Insert (Windows) or Open (Mac).

5 Click Ignore when a warning message asks if you want to overwrite existing styles. This message appears because both files include the same styles. Styles are prebuilt combinations of special effects that can be added to vector graphics.

A new page is added and uses the same page name as you saw in the Import Page dialog box.

6 Select the actor_view_wendy page, if necessary.

7 Repeat steps 1–5, this time importing the actor_view_vitto page.

The final page is added to the file.

8 Choose File > Save As. Name the file cast_navigator_working.fw.png.

▶ **Tip:** You can also move between pages by choosing a new page from the page navigator list, located near the top right of the document window.

● **Note:** As you change the order, the sequence numbers of the second and third pages also change. By default, Fireworks automatically changes the page numbers based on their stacking order, from top to bottom. To turn off numbering, choose Numbering from the Pages panel menu.

Photoshop and multipage Fireworks files

While you can save a Fireworks document as a Photoshop file (PSD), this only saves the currently active page, as Photoshop has no way of interpreting multiple pages within a single document.

If you need to return to Photoshop, you can do one of the following:

- Export pages to files: Choose File > Export, and choose Pages to Files from the Export List. This produces a flattened PNG of the first state each page.

- Save as a Photoshop file: Choose File > Save As and choose Photoshop from the Save as Type menu. This produces an editable, layered Photoshop file of the currently selected page and state.

Note: To learn more about pages and creating links between them, read Lesson 10.

Doug Hungarter has written a free extension called Convert Pages to PSD, which allows you to export all the pages in a Fireworks document as separate PSD files. To learn more about this extension, visit the Adobe Exchange: www.adobe.com/cfusion/exchange/index.cfm?event=extensionDetail&loc=en_us&extid=1849527#.

Working with layers

Tip: Fireworks highlights independent objects as you move the mouse over them. As your mouse glides over objects on the canvas, different areas are highlighted in red. This highlight indicates the independent object in that particular spot; you can then click to select that specific object.

In this and the following sections, you'll continue to work with the cast_navigator_working.fw.png file to see layers at work.

Naming objects

A good habit to develop is giving your objects meaningful names.

1 Select the home_double_identity page and then switch to the Layers panel by clicking the Layers tab.

2 To see more of the Layers panel, and to minimize the need for scrolling, collapse the other visible panel groups by double-clicking the gray tab bar next to the panel names in other (non-Layers) panel groups.

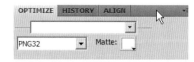

Note: In the rush to create a file, you may overlook this essential part of structuring your document. But when passing a file onto a co-worker, a document full of unnamed objects and layers can be very hard to navigate and make sense of.

3 Select the photo of the actor on the canvas.

4 In the Layers panel, double-click on the highlighted object called—none too descriptively—Bitmap.

5 Rename it to **Cast thumbnail**.

6 Click on the second thumbnail image on the canvas, and rename it **Auction thumbnail**.

7 Click on the third thumbnail image on the canvas, the group, and rename it **RSS thumbnail: 2 objects**.

8 Proceed to rename the other objects, in this order, from the top down, as follows:

- RSS text
- Cast text
- Auction text
- RSS heading
- Cast heading
- Auction heading
- RSS background
- Cast background
- Auction background
- Cast thumbnail (already named)
- Close button
- Logo: 2 objects
- Bottom panel highlight
- Top panel highlight
- Panel background
- Panel shadow

Rearranging objects in a layer

After the previous exercise, it should be pretty obvious that objects are, well, all over the place in this design! Let's add some structure first by rearranging some of the objects.

1 Select the Cast thumbnail object in the Layers panel.

2 Drag it upward to the top of Layer 1 in the panel.

3 Choose File > Save to save your work so far.

Note: Dragging an object to the top of a layer can be tricky; if you can't seem to place it at the top, it will most likely drop in as the second from the top image. At that point, simply drag the Auction thumbnail object below the Cast thumbnail object.

Adding and naming layers

Things are a little more organized now. To help structure the file even more, you will add a new layer to the Layers panel.

1 Click the New/Duplicate Layer button at the bottom of the Layers panel. A new layer, appropriately called Layer 2, appears above the existing layer.

2 Double-click the new Layer 2 in the Layers panel, and change its name to **Content**.

3 Double-click the original Layer 1, and rename it **Interface**.

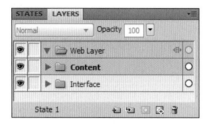

Moving objects from one layer to another

Now that you have a Content layer, you can fill it with—you guessed it—content.

1 In the Interface layer, click the Cast thumbnail object.

2 Scroll down until you see the second Auction background object.

3 Hold down the Shift key and select this object. All objects from Cast thumbnail to Auction background are now selected.

4 Drag the selected objects into the Content layer. The easiest way to do this is to drag the radio button from the Interface layer onto the radio button on the Content layer.

Now all the content is in its own layer, and the interface items are in their own layer.

● **Note:** You can also cut selected objects, select a new layer, and paste the objects, or you can click and drag an object (or a series of selected objects) to a different layer.

▶ **Tip:** To select objects that aren't directly above or below each other, press Ctrl (Windows) or Command (Mac) as you select them.

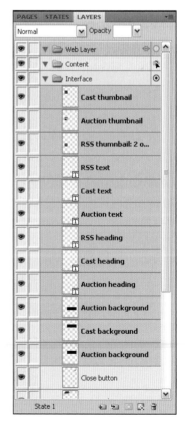

Creating sublayers

For additional structure, you can use sublayers to contain related content in a single layer.

1 Make sure the Content layer is selected.

2 Click the New Sub Layer button at the bottom of the Layers panel to add a sublayer in the Content layer.

3 Rename this new sublayer **Hide Me**.

4 Shift-click to select the RSS text through Auction heading objects—a total of six objects.

5 Drag the radio button from the Content layer onto the radio button on the Hide Me layer to move these six text objects.

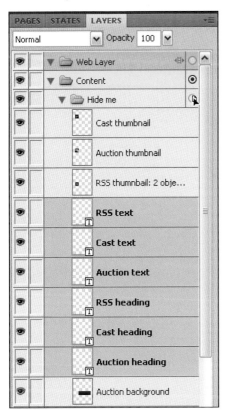

6 Click the Expand/Collapse Layer icon to collapse the Hide Me sublayer. If the text objects disappear from view in the panel, you know they are in the right place.

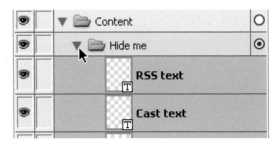

● **Note:** Often you will place text content into a design for placement or layout purposes only. The Fireworks text is not expected to be used beyond this design stage. By placing this content into a layer of its own, you can quickly hide the content from view. By naming the layer Hide Me, you make it obvious that this content is only temporary.

7 Click the Expand/Collapse Layer icons to minimize the Content and Interface layers. You can see how much more manageable this design has become.

8 Save your work.

With these few simple steps, this page is far more organized. You can easily expand or collapse the individual layers in the Layers panel to display only the objects you need to work on.

Protecting layers

When a layer is locked, no object within it can be selected or deleted by accident.

1 Click the Lock column in the Interface layer.

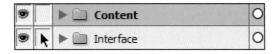

2 Expand the Interface layer. Notice the ghost of a lock appears beside each object.

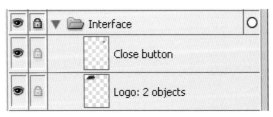

3 Try to select one of the objects in the Interface layer. You can't, because they are all locked.

If your concern is only to protect certain objects rather than the entire layer, you can do that, too:

4 Right-click (Windows) or Control-click (Mac) the layer in the Layers panel.

5 Choose Unlock All from the context menu.

6 Lock the objects named Bottom panel highlight, Panel shadow, Panel background, and Panel outline.

7 On the canvas, hover over the logo and the Close button. Red highlights indicate those objects are selectable.

8 Hover over the bottom of the panel. No red indicators appear. These objects are locked.

9 Unlock the objects individually by selecting the lock icon beside each object name.

10 Save the file.

| New Image |
| New Layer... |
| New Sub Layer... |
| Duplicate Layer... |
| Share Layer To States |
| Single Layer Editing |
| Delete Layer |
| Add Master Page Layer |
| Share Layer To Pages... |
| Share Layer To All Pages |
| Exclude Shared Layer |
| Detach Shared Layer |
| Flatten Selection |
| Merge Down |
| Hide All |
| Show All |
| Lock All |
| Unlock All |
| Add Mask |
| Edit Mask |
| Disable Mask |
| Delete Mask |
| Thumbnail Options... |
| Help |

Layer options

Like many panels in Fireworks, the Layers panel has options for configuring the panel, adding new layers or sublayers, and determining how a layer interacts with other pages or states within a Fireworks design.

Access the Layers panel's options by right-clicking (or Control-clicking) any layer or by opening the Layers panel menu in the top-right corner of the panel ( ).

Among other options, you can increase the size of thumbnails by selecting Thumbnail Options to make the images easier to recognize.

Working with states

States are an important part of Fireworks. They can be used for mocking up Web site interaction (rollovers, Ajax emulation), or to show how an application may change based on user input.

The cast navigator file is a mockup of a planned AIR application. To give the user a real sense of how the application would behave, a separate state has been added to show what happens when a user hovers over or clicks on certain areas of the application. This design is still in its early stage—the interactivity has yet to be added by using slices and hotspots—but you will add a second state to the main page to add the rollover effects.

Duplicating and naming states

You will need various parts of the interface for the rollover effects. The simplest way to add those parts to a second state is to duplicate the existing one.

1   Select the States tab.

2   Drag the State 1 to the New/Duplicate state icon near the bottom right of the States panel. This creates a duplicate state, including all the assets and layer hierarchy.

3   Double-click on the State 1 name and rename it **Up**.

4   Rename State 2 **Over**.

Changing content on states

Let's examine these two states more closely.

1   Select the Layers panel.

    The currently selected state is displayed at the bottom-left corner of the Layers panel.

2   Click on Current State and choose the Over state from the pop-up menu.

3   Use the Pointer tool to select the Close button.

> **Tip:** States can include completely different content, or they can just indicate changes to certain elements that appear in both states. For example, a button may display a glow or drop shadow in a second state.

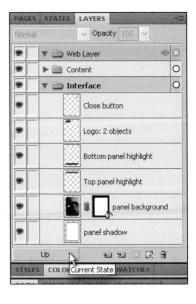

4 In the Properties panel, click the plus sign next to Filters, and choose Shadow And Glow > Glow.

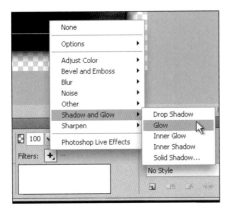

5 Set the values as seen in this graphic: Distance: 0, Opacity: 100, Color: #DF0000, Softness: 12, Offset: 0.

6 Click away from the Filter Properties box to lock in the changes.

7 Toggle back and forth between the Up and Over states to compare the differences.

8 Make sure the Over state is selected.

9 Holding down Shift, click on the thumbnails and the background rectangles for all three categories (Cast Members, Auction, and RSS). If you select the text accidentally, simply click on it again while holding Shift and it will be deselected.

10 In the Properties panel, select the "i" icon beside the Photoshop Live Effects filter in the current filter list. The Photoshop Live Effects dialog box opens.

11 Select the Stroke option on the left. Change the Fill Color property to #FFFFFF (white).

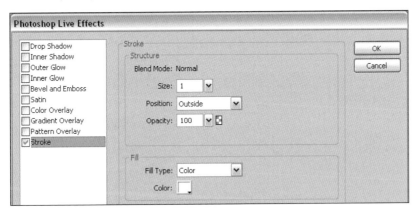

Note: Fireworks includes Photoshop Live Effects primarily so you can continue to edit Photoshop layer styles in Fireworks. However, the Photoshop Live Effects dialog box isn't as robust as the Layer Styles dialog box in Photoshop.

Adding multiple live filters

The great thing about live filters is that you can have multiple filters applied to a single object. You'll add three filters to the movie title object in the Up state.

Select the Up state from the Layers panel.

1   Select the movie title.

2   In the Properties panel, choose Adjust Color > Levels. The Levels dialog box appears.

3   From left to right, set the Input levels to 0, 1, and 206 and click OK.

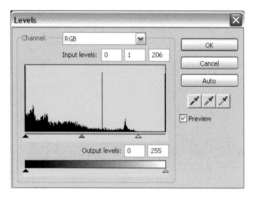

4   Choose Shadow And Glow > Glow and set the values as follows: Distance: 0, Opacity: 22, Color: #FFFFFF, Softness: 11, Offset: 0.

Note: To learn more about Web slices and optimizing graphics, read Lesson 8. To learn more about states and interactivity, read Lessons 10 and 11.

5   Click away from the Properties panel to lock in the settings.

6   Toggle back and forth between the two states to see the differences to the mockup.

7   Save the file.

Extra credit

In this lesson, you've learned some of the key features of working with pages, states, and layers. You have more than one page in this design, though! Based on this lesson's exercises, try to restructure the other pages, layers, and states in a similar manner.

As a Web or interactive designer, you will use these Fireworks elements on a regular basis, so a little practice is a good idea.

Review questions

1 What is the importance of layers?

2 What special layer does every Fireworks document have?

3 Name two benefits of using pages.

4 How do you move objects from one layer to another?

5 What are states used for?

Review answers

1 Layers add structure to your document.

   As you add more objects to a design, it becomes harder to locate specific images or text areas because you have to scroll through a very long list. With objects sorted into multiple layers, you can quickly collapse layers to see your main design structure or expand a specific layer to select an individual object. Layers also allow objects to be independent from one another. You can add or remove layers or the objects within them without affecting other elements in the design. You can change how objects within layers interact with other layers by changing the stacking order of layers.

2 Every Fireworks document has a Web layer. This is where interactive elements called hotspots and slices are stored. The Web layer does not have to be used in a design, but it cannot be deleted.

3 Pages let you create a variety of designs within a single file. This improves asset management, because unique designs for one project can all be stored in the same file. Pages can also be linked using hotspots or slices to create a truly interactive experience for testing and proof of concept.

4 You can move objects in one of several ways within the Layers panel:

   • Cut and paste a selected object from one layer to another.

   • Drag a selected object or objects from layer to layer.

   • Select an object or objects within one layer, and drag the associated radio button from the original layer to the radio button on the target layer.

5 States can be used to create simple frame-based animation, or to show changes in the appearance of interactive elements, such as buttons. States can also display completely different content within the same page.

3 WORKING WITH BITMAP IMAGES

Lesson overview

In this lesson, you'll learn how to do the following:

- Select and use some of the bitmap tools in the Tools panel

- Open and import bitmap images in Fireworks

- Use a variety of methods to crop images

- Set options for a selected tool using the Properties panel

- Use guides to help position and align images

- Use the 9-slice Scaling tool to scale bitmap images

- Use various bitmap tools and filters to adjust brightness, contrast, and tonality of bitmap images

- Correct images using the Rubber Stamp tool

- Align objects on the canvas using the Align panel

 This lesson takes approximately 90 minutes to complete. Copy the Lesson03 folder into the Lessons folder that you created on your hard drive for these projects (or create it now, if you haven't already done so). As you work on this lesson, you won't be preserving the start files; if you need to restore the start files, copy them from the *Adobe Fireworks CS5 Classroom in a Book* CD.

Everyone enjoys surfing through a good-looking
website or using a professionally designed interface.
Adobe Fireworks includes a solid set of tools for
creating and editing bitmap images.

Resolution and file size

Image resolution and file size are directly related to each other. The greater the number of pixels in an image, the larger the file size will be. We're not talking about the printed size of an image here; we're dealing specifically with the number of pixels that make up an image. For example, many current digital cameras will capture an image consisting of 3000 pixels horizontally by 2000 pixels vertically (or greater). Do the math, and you'll quickly see that an image with this resolution contains 6 million pixels in total and weighs in at about **23 MB**.

The higher the capture resolution, the larger the file size will be.

Image resolution vs. image quality

Resolution and *quality* are two different things; you can have a high-resolution image that doesn't look very good, due to poor quality in the original scan or heavy image compression that might be set on a digital camera. *Resolution* refers to the actual number of pixels that make up the image, not the empirical or subjective quality of the image.

Tips for working with bitmaps

Good-quality graphics are key assets to many professional websites. The image-editing and layout tools in Fireworks give you the freedom to do most—if not all—of your bitmap work without leaving the application.

That said, you should keep a couple of caveats in mind:

- The maximum canvas-creation size in Fireworks is 6000 x 6000 pixels. You can work on files that are larger than this, but 6000 x 6000 pixels is the largest that you can create within the program.

- Fireworks was designed to work with graphics destined for screen use, and it's here that its speed and flexibility really shine. While you can open and work on very high-resolution files in Fireworks, you may find the application begins to get sluggish over time. And you may not want to have several of these files open at the same time.

Cropping an image

Cropping is a common way to remove extraneous detail, letting you focus more exclusively on a specific part of an image. In this exercise, you will remove surrounding detail in a photo to help focus on just the actor's face.

1   Choose File > Open, and browse to the file Mark_actor06.jpg in the Lesson03 folder on your hard drive. Click Open.

2   Select the Crop tool from the Tools panel.

3   Click and drag a box around the face of the actor. Include the hat and part of the tie.

4   Press Enter or Return to crop the image.

Hmm, looks like we got a bit too close to the collar. We'd better go back.

5   Press Ctrl+Z (Windows) or Command+Z (Mac) to undo the crop.

6   Making sure the Crop tool is still selected, draw the crop one more time, leaving a bit more space on the sides.

▶ **Tip:** If you change your mind about cropping at all, you can press the Escape key to cancel the action.

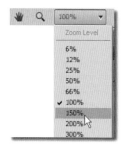

7 Move the cursor to the middle control handle on the bottom of the image, and drag it up. Stop when the crop line touches the upper red stripe in the actor's tie.

8 Press Enter or Return to commit to the crop.

9 Choose File > Close, and don't save the file when you are prompted.

Cropping a single bitmap image in a design

Cropping single images is fine, but what if you need to crop an image that's already on a layer in a design? Fireworks offers a way to do this as well.

1 Open watch_promo.fw.png from the Lesson03 folder.

2 Choose 150 from the Zoom Level menu on the Application bar to zoom in to 150%.

3 Use the Pointer tool ( ) to select the watch.

4 Choose Edit > Crop Selected Bitmap. Crop marks will appear around the watch image.

5 Drag the top and bottom crop marks so that only the watch face is inside the crop.

6 Press Enter or Return to commit to the crop.

Managing images on the canvas

When you have more than one image or object on the canvas, Fireworks gives you a variety of ways to work with those images, from showing and hiding objects to positioning and grouping them. You'll find that steps like these are a common part of most design workflows.

Adjusting the watch position

To experiment with this feature, you'll adjust the position of the watch image you've already got open. Because you are dealing with exact measurements here, you need to be aware of the exact *x* and *y* coordinates of the image.

1   Select the watch with the Pointer tool, and check the values for *x* and *y* in the Properties panel. The watch should be positioned at X: 30, Y: 135.

2   If the watch is not in position, use the arrow keys on the keyboard to move the image one pixel at a time.

▶ **Tip:** To nudge a selected object 10 pixels at a time, hold down the Shift key as you press the arrow keys. You can also change a selected object's position by entering new values in the Properties panel.

Hiding and locking objects

With the watch cropped, there's no need for that large ellipse, so let's hide it from view for now.

1   In the Layers panel, locate and select the ellipse.

2   Lock the ellipse object in the Layers panel by clicking the empty box beside the eye icon. Locking the object prevents you from accidentally selecting it.

3   Click the eye icon to hide the ellipse from view.

To give the design a grittier feel, you're also going to replace the gradient backdrop with a bitmap image, so we'll set up for that now.

4   Hide the gradient rectangle by clicking its eye icon in the Layers panel.

5   Lock the rectangle in the Layers panel by clicking the empty box beside the eye icon.

Working with guides

In this exercise, you will use guides to help ensure an exact position and height between the canvas and an image you will import into the design. Guides are great tools for aligning and placing objects on the canvas.

1 If rulers are not visible, choose View > Rulers.

2 Move the cursor to the ruler at the left of the window.

3 Click and drag toward the canvas. A vertical guide appears. You will also see a tooltip appear beside the guide, with an x value. (If you don't see the tooltip, choose View > Tooltips.) This value is the horizontal position of the vertical guide.

Note: The right and bottom guides will not display on a Mac but objects will still behave correctly in proximity to them—snapping to guides, showing distances between guides, and so forth.

4 When the tooltip displays 0, release the mouse. The guide drops at that location.

5 Drag in another vertical guide, and place it at 500.

6 Drag guides from the top ruler to these positions: 0 and 500. If you need to reposition guides, you can simply select them with the Pointer tool and drag them to a new position. Doing so effectively boxes in the canvas.

Importing images

A very quick way to add existing images to a design is to *import* them onto the canvas. You will add your new background image this way. Importing gives you the ability to scale the image proportionately when you add it to the canvas.

1 Zoom out to 66% using either the Zoom tool in the Tools panel or the Zoom Level menu in the Application bar.

2 Choose File > Import.

3 Browse to the Lesson03 folder, and locate the promo_backdrop.jpg file.

4 Click Open.

Tip: When importing, if you simply click the mouse button without dragging, the image will be imported at its full height and width, with its top-left corner positioned at the import cursor's location.

Back on the canvas, you'll notice that the cursor has changed to an inverted L shape ( ). This is the import cursor. If you click and drag the mouse, you will begin to draw a marquee. If you release the mouse button, your image will be imported at the dimensions you've created via the marquee, based on the height-to-width (aspect) ratio of the original image. If you simply click the mouse button without dragging, the image will be imported at its full height and width, with its top-left corner where you clicked.

5 Place the cursor in the upper-left corner of the canvas, and then click and drag toward the lower-right side of the canvas.

You will notice from the marquee guideline that in order to get the image to cover the full width of the canvas, it's actually going to be too tall. This will result in a portion of the image being cut off. For the purpose of this exercise, you will want the entire image to fit within the height of your canvas, regardless of its width.

6 Drag the cursor up so that the height of the image fits within the canvas area. The cursor should snap to the bottom guide when you get within five pixels of it. When you release the mouse, the image will appear (a foggy alleyway), but, as noted earlier, it doesn't cover the full width of the canvas.

7 Check the Properties panel to ensure that the x and y positions of the image you imported are both at 0, and press Ctrl+S (Windows) or Command+S (Mac) to save your changes.

Distortion-free bitmap scaling

Scaling objects in one direction—whether they are bitmap images or vector shapes —can cause unwanted distortion. Take, for example, the image you just imported. Traditional scaling will distort the entire image, giving you an undesirable result. But Fireworks has a great feature called 9-slice scaling that eliminates distortion. You could use the Scale tool, but in the first exercise, you'll see its limitations.

Scaling the "old" way

You'll use the Scale tool to scale the backdrop image.

1 Make sure the backdrop image is still active—look for the blue control handles at the four corners of the shape. If you don't see them, use the Pointer tool to select the image on the canvas.

2 Select the Scale tool () from the Tools panel.

   Control handles appear around the rectangle.

3 Drag the right-middle control handle straight out to the right side of the canvas.

4 Release the mouse button, and note how the image is stretched and somewhat distorted. It can definitely be better!

5 Press the Escape key to cancel the transformation.

Avoiding distortion with the 9-slice Scaling tool

If a bitmap image contains an area that doesn't have a lot of detail (a very important point to note), you can use the 9-slice Scaling tool to make the image fit with no noticeable damage.

1 Make sure the backdrop image is still selected.

2 Select the 9-slice Scaling tool from the Tools panel (▣). The scaling handles appear again, but the image is now divided with special 9-slice guides. These guides can be positioned prior to scaling, and anything that is outside the guides will remain unchanged during a scaling operation.

3 Move the cursor over the vertical 9-slice guide on the left.

4 When the cursor changes to a double-headed arrow, drag the guide in the image to the area of fog that has no noticeable detail.

5 Position the right-side 9-slice guide in the fog as well, similar to what you see here. Watch out for those puddles in the foreground of the photo! The position of the horizontal guides is not important for this example.

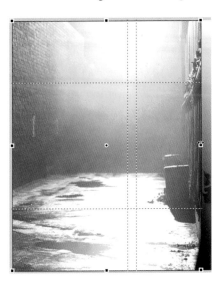

6 Drag the right-middle control handle out to 500 pixels. Tooltips do not display when using the 9-slice guides, so watch the top ruler to make sure you have reached the 500-pixel distance.

7 Release the mouse button. Only the areas enclosed by the 9-slice guides (areas with no real detail) were scaled (stretched). The sides of the image, where the puddles and garbage gave the image detail and definition, were not stretched.

You now have an image that actually fits the canvas! Press Enter to accept the transformation.

8 If the watch and investigator images are hidden by the new background, drag them up in the stacking order in the Layers panel (or choose Modify > Arrange > Send To Back to move the alley scene to the bottom of the pile of images).

9 Press Ctrl+S (Windows) or Command+S (Mac) to save your work.

Adjusting tonal range

The background image you've imported adds a certain air of mystery to the design, but it's a bit low in contrast, lacking visual impact. You will use a Live Filter to adjust the contrast.

1 Ensure the alleyway photo is selected (look for that blue bounding box), and then click the plus sign (+) in the Filters area of the Properties panel.

2 Choose Adjust Color > Levels. The Levels dialog box appears.

The histogram (graph) in the Levels dialog box shows you the distribution of tones in the selected image; you use it to alter shadows, midtones, and highlights. Directly below the histogram are the input level sliders: shadows on the left, highlights on the right, and midtones in the middle.

In this image, you'll notice that there is nothing displaying in the histogram for the darker tones.

3 Drag the left slider to the right so that it almost lines up with the beginning of the histogram chart. The Input value should read about 90, as seen here.

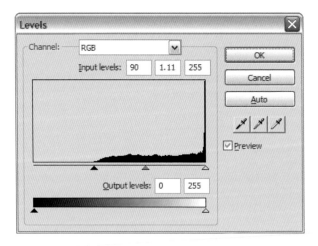

What Are Live Filters?

Live Filters are nondestructive effects you can apply to most objects (vector, bitmap, or symbol) within Fireworks. The great power and advantage of Live Filters is that you can always edit the effect at a later time. If you feel the filter is too harsh, or too subtle, just click the "i" icon to edit the filter properties. Note that this icon becomes available once the Live Filter has been added to the Properties panel.

4 Lighten the midtones slightly by dragging the middle slider to the left, for an input value of 1.11. Click OK.

   The Levels Live Filter now appears in the Filters list in the Properties panel.

   The result is definitely an improvement, but now things are a little too dark in the shadows and a bit too bright in the midtones. You will reopen the Levels filter and make further adjustments.

5 Click the "i" icon next to the Levels filter in the Live Filters category of the Properties panel. The Levels dialog box reopens.

6 Change the shadow input value to **80** by typing the numbers into the leftmost input box above the histogram.

7 Change the midtone value back to **1** by changing the value in the middle input box. Click OK.

8 Press Ctrl+S (Windows) or Command+S (Mac) to save your work.

Using the Align panel

Guides and Smart Guides are helpful for positioning items, but they're "one object at a time" features. If you have multiple items you need to reposition, the Align panel is the tool to use.

In this exercise, you will add four more watches to show the available color range of the product. You can import each file one at a time if you like (tan_, green_, blue_, and magenta_watch.jpg), but to make things a little easier for you, we have provided a single Fireworks PNG file that contains all four watches, and that is the one you will use in this exercise.

1 Choose File > Import.

2 Browse to the Lesson03 folder, and select the watch_colors.fw.png file.

   Unlike the cast_navigator_assets.fw.png file from Lesson 2, this is just a single-page Fireworks PNG file. There are no additional pages to browse through.

3 Click Open. The Import Page dialog box appears.

4 Make sure **Insert after current page** is not selected and then click Import (Windows) or Open (Mac).

5 Click anywhere on the canvas to import the collection of images at their original sizes. You can see things are a bit messy, much like how it would look if you quickly dragged and dropped the images from another document window.

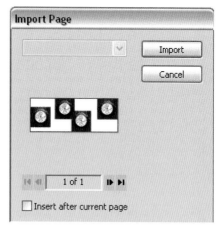

In the Layers panel, notice that each image is truly a separate object. This is one of the beauties of a Fireworks PNG; because each image was a unique object in the original PNG file, each is imported as a separate, unique object.

All four objects should still be selected. If not, use the Shift key and click on each watch in turn to select them all.

6 Open the Align panel (choose Window > Align if you don't see the Align panel tab in your Panel groups).

7 Click the Align Top Edge button to align the top edges of all the objects.

8 Change the Space menu option to a value of **10**, instead of the default option of Evenly.

9 Click the Space Evenly Horizontally icon right above the Space menu. You now have a nice, neat, evenly spaced row of watches. Don't worry if the watches aren't all fully on your canvas; we'll deal with that in the next exercise.

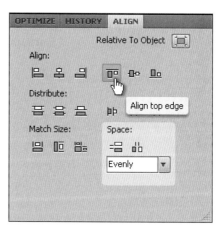

10 Press Ctrl+S (Windows) or Command+S (Mac) to save your work.

Grouping objects together

The canvas is starting to fill up with several graphics. You're going to make your life a little easier by grouping that row of watches together. Grouping temporarily turns a series of selected objects into a single object, making it easier to manipulate them.

1   Make sure the four watches are still selected.

2   Choose Modify > Group.

In the Layers panel, you will see that the four watches are now part of the same object, with a new name of Group: 4 Objects.

3   Select the Pointer tool, and, if necessary, drag the group to the left edge of the main watch. Smart Guides—the purple dashed lines that appear and disappear as you move one object around the edges of other objects on your canvas—will help you get this adjustment just right.

The row of watches takes up a fair amount of space and may overlap the investigator image. You will scale the group using a new feature in the Properties panel to make it fit the layout better.

4   Click the hollow square to the left of the width and height. The square becomes solid and you have now constrained the proportions of the group.

5   Type **344** into the Width field and then press the Tab key. The height is automatically scaled to proportionately match the width.

6   In the Properties panel, set the x value to **28** and the y value to **398**, so the group of watches is below the main watch.

7   Press Ctrl+S (Windows) or Command+S (Mac) to save your work.

> **Tip:** You can also choose Modify > Transform > Numeric Transform, to scale by percentage, resize by exact pixels, or rotate an object to a specific angle.

Adjusting brightness with the Dodge and Burn tools

Sometimes a photo has good general exposure but there are areas in the image that are too light or too dark. These areas need some local adjustment, and this is where the Dodge and Burn tools come in handy.

The Dodge and Burn tools are part of the bitmap-retouching toolset; their effects are permanent (sometimes called "destructive") in that the tools completely alter pixel values. As we go along in this exercise, you will also learn how to protect your original image.

1   Choose File > Open, and browse for the detective.jpg file in the Lesson03 folder.

2   Click Open.

This image is in pretty good shape, but the subject's face is a bit too dark and his white shirt a bit too bright. You'll use the Dodge and Burn tools to correct this.

3   To keep your original safe, make a copy of the photo by dragging its thumbnail down to the New Bitmap Image icon in the Layers panel.

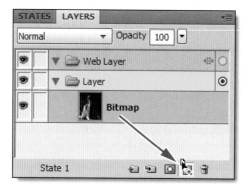

4   Double-click the word Bitmap next to the selected image in the Layers panel, and rename it **Retouch**. This will help you to differentiate between the two images with a quick glance at the Layers panel at any time.

5   Use the Zoom tool to magnify the subject's face.

Now we're ready to delve into the different uses of the two specific tools.

> **Tip:** Rather than adjusting the zoom level from the Application bar or menus and then having to reposition the image focus on the detective's face, you'll find it easiest to use the Zoom tool to drag a marquee around the face. When you release the mouse, Fireworks automatically centers the selected area on the canvas, and you're ready to go.

Lightening with the Dodge tool

Dodging—an old photo darkroom term for making specific areas of a photo brighter—has been carried over into a variety of bitmap-editing software. The Dodge tool lightens up local areas of an image by painting over the area.

1   Select the Dodge tool from the Tools panel.

2   In the Properties panel, change Size to **48**. Make sure Edge is set to **100** (for a soft-edged brush), Shape to Circular, Range to Shadow, and Exposure to **6**.

Note: Dodging and burning are more realistic if the exposures are set to low values and then reapplied if necessary. If you find the changes you're making to be too subtle, you can paint over the area a second time—or more, if you prefer.

3   Carefully paint over the actor's face and neck without releasing the mouse. Avoid painting over the hat. Because you have chosen Shadows as the range, you can safely paint over the bright areas of his face without concern.

4   Press Ctrl+Z (Windows) or Command+Z (Mac) to undo the editing, and compare the original with the lightened version. The effect is subtle, but noticeable.

If you find the effect too subtle, you can paint over the area again.

5   Press Ctrl+Y (Windows) or Command+Y (Mac) to reapply the dodging.

Darkening with the Burn tool

The Burn tool does the exact opposite of the Dodge tool; it darkens specific areas when it is applied.

1   Switch to the Burn tool.

2   In the Properties panel, change Size to **33**, Range to Midtones, and Exposure to **15**. Leave Edge and Shape the same (100 and Circular).

3   Paint over the bright area on the actor's cheek.

Burning in will add exposure, making the cheek slightly darker. This should give an appearance of more evenly applied lighting to the detective's face, instead of one side being significantly lighter or darker than the other.

Now we'll alter the shirt slightly to complete the changes this image needs.

4   Set the Zoom level to 100% again.

If you find the effect too subtle, you can paint over the area again.

5   Change Size to **60**, Range to Highlights, and Exposure to **8**. You don't have to change the Shape and Edge settings.

6   Without releasing the mouse button, paint over the white shirt sleeve and shirt on the left side of the image. Notice how the shirt gets somewhat darker.

Tip: A quick way to get to 100 percent magnification is to press Ctrl+1 (Windows) or Command+1 (Mac) or simply double-click the Zoom tool in the Tools panel.

7   Hide the upper copy of the image by clicking its eye icon in the Layers panel to compare the original with the altered image. Although each of the changes we made was small, the overall effect on the image is quite substantial.

8   Continue to alter the image if you like, or simply save the file by pressing Ctrl+S (Windows) or Command+S (Mac).

Applying the Unsharp Mask Live Filter

When resizing an image (often called *resampling*), pixels are added or removed from the file. When you resize an image to larger than its original size, you are adding pixels and increasing the file size. Generally this *upsampling* is not recommended in Fireworks unless it is only by a small percentage or for special effect, because the image quality can degrade noticeably. When you make an image smaller (*downsampling*), you are removing pixel data from the image and reducing the file size. This tends to make the image softer, but we can gain back some of the original crispness of the photo by applying a filter called Unsharp Mask. Unsharp Mask can be applied as either a permanent filter or as a Live Filter. For the greatest flexibility, Live Filters are a better option.

1   Choose File > Open, and select the policeman.jpg file in the Lesson03 folder.

2   Select the Open As Untitled option at the bottom of the dialog box. (This will open an untitled copy of the image.)

3   Click Open.

When the file opens, it is quite large—4368 x 2912 pixels in size. This is one of the high-resolution images from the movie photo shoot and is much too large for use on the Web. You will resize it to a more suitable dimension and resolution.

4   Choose Modify > Canvas > Image Size to launch the Image Size dialog box.

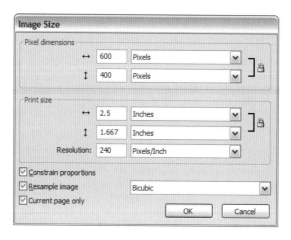

5 Make sure the Constrain Proportions option is checked.

6 Set the width to 600 pixels and press Tab. The height will automatically change based on the width you have entered.

7 Click OK. After you resize the image, double-click the Zoom tool or press Ctrl+1 (Windows) or Command+1 (Mac) to bring it to 100%.

8 Click the Add Live Filters icon (+ sign) in the Properties panel.

9 Choose Sharpen > Unsharp Mask to open the Unsharp Mask dialog box. The default properties are a bit extreme for a low-resolution file, so we'll alter one slightly.

10 Change the Pixel Radius to a value of **1**.

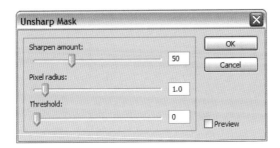

11 Deselect the Preview option to see the image without sharpening.

12 Activate Preview again. Notice that there is slightly more contrast and even a bit better separation between the officer and the background. This is because Unsharp Mask increases the contrast only of *edge pixels* (the place where a dark and light pixel meet).

13 Click OK to apply the filter.

Unsharp Mask Properties

Generally, higher-resolution images can handle (and sometimes need) higher amounts of unsharp-masking than low-resolution images. The three controls for the Unsharp Masking filter are the following:

- Sharpen Amount: This property controls how much darker and lighter the edge borders become. Sharpen Amount can also be thought of as how much contrast is added at the edges.

- Pixel Radius: This property affects the size of the edges to be sharpened. A smaller radius enhances smaller-scale detail. Higher radius values can cause halos at the edges (a highlight around objects), making images look unnatural. Fine detail needs a smaller radius value. Pixel Radius and Sharpen Amount are reciprocal; reducing one allows more of the other.

- Threshold: This property controls how far apart adjacent tonal values have to be before the filter does anything. The threshold setting can be used to sharpen more pronounced edges while ignoring more subtle edges. Low values have a greater effect because fewer areas are excluded. Higher threshold values exclude areas of lower contrast.

Repairing areas with the Rubber Stamp tool

Fireworks is not Photoshop. There—we've said it. If you have large images that require major manipulation, chances are you should do that kind of heavy-duty work in Photoshop first. Every job has a correct tool. That said, Fireworks comes with a decent set of standard retouching tools, including the Rubber Stamp tool ( ). These tools can handle most basic retouching requirements. The Rubber Stamp (also known as the Clone Stamp) tool copies pixel detail from one location in a bitmap image and pastes it into another (presumably damaged or unsightly) area. Maybe there is a scratch in some packaging or a fly-away thread in some clothing. Maybe you need to smooth out skin tones in a photo or remove an unwanted highlight in a shiny object. These are all good examples of when to use the Rubber Stamp tool.

Here are the general steps to using the Rubber Stamp tool:

1 Click an area to designate it as the source (the area you want to clone). The sampling pointer becomes a crosshair pointer.

Note: To designate a different area of pixels to clone, Alt-click (Windows) or Option-click (Mac) another area of pixels.

2 Move to a different part of the image, and drag the pointer. Two pointers appear. The first is the source and is in the shape of a crosshair. Depending on the brush preferences you've selected, the second pointer is a rubber stamp, a crosshair, or a blue circle. As you drag the second pointer, pixels beneath the first pointer are copied and applied to the area beneath the second.

▶ **Tip:** You can change the cursor display for many editing tools by choosing Edit > Preferences (Windows) or Fireworks > Preferences (Mac) and then selecting the Edit category. Select or deselect the cursor options to change how the cursor is represented.

Now you will test this process. In the file we'll open, the overall image is fine, but there are some distracting wrinkles in the sofa cushion where the actor is seated. You're going to smooth over that area using the Rubber Stamp tool.

1 Choose File > Open, and select the Mark_actor02.jpg file in the Lesson03 folder.

2 Click Open.

3 Zoom in, as described earlier in the chapter, to focus in on the cushion area. When retouching, it's always good to get close to your subject matter.

4 Select the Rubber Stamp tool from the Bitmap tools area of the Tools panel.

Notice that the Properties panel updates, displaying attributes for the Rubber Stamp tool. You can set the brush size and the edge softness of the brush (100 is soft, 0 is hard). You can also decide whether you want to keep your brush aligned with the original source of sampling and if you want to sample from all the layers/objects in your document, or just the active object.

5 In the Properties panel, set your brush size to **28** pixels and the edge to 100%. Leave the Opacity setting at 100.

6 Deselect the Source Aligned option. This will ensure that the sampling always begins at the same source point, no matter where you begin your actual rubber-stamping.

7 Locate an area on the cushion that is mostly smooth and similar in brightness to the wrinkled area. Hold down Alt (Windows) or Option (Mac), and click to sample the pixels from this area.

8 Move the cursor over to the beginning of the wrinkled area.

9 Click and hold the mouse button, and then begin painting carefully over the area. Continue painting until the large wrinkles are gone. Some variation in tone is fine; you want the retouching to look as realistic as possible. If necessary, release the mouse button and repeat the process to get farther to the right or lower down in the wrinkles. Because the Rubber Stamp tool duplicates the exact pixels, the texture and tone of the leather remain visible.

> **Tip:** If you notice that the area you are cloning seems much too light or dark, stop stamping, press Ctrl+Z (Windows) or Command+Z (Mac) to undo the painting, and resample (Alt-click on Windows or Option-click on Mac) from a more suitable area.

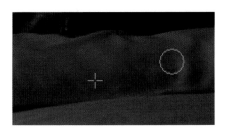

Retouching on a separate bitmap object

Cloning as we've described is a permanent (destructive) process; you are literally replacing pixels in one area with pixels from another. If you save and close the file, those changes become a part of the image.

Many professionals prefer to do this type of retouching on a separate layer. In this way, they avoid the potential for permanently ruining (or even just changing) an original image. Fireworks lets you do this kind of work in an empty bitmap object, even in the same layer as the original artwork.

Look at the actor's face. He's got a couple of creases on his forehead, which make him look a little older and more tired than perhaps he really is. You are going to retouch those wrinkles as a separate object, first creating the necessary empty bitmap object. This way, you can show or hide the wrinkles, depending on your plans for the image.

An empty bitmap object is an area containing no pixel data. It gives you the opportunity to add new pixel information as a separate, unique object. Once you create this object, you must add pixel data to it in your next step, or the object will be removed from the Layers panel. You might use this object if you are planning to use the Brush or Pencil tools to add colored bitmap lines. In this case, we'll be using it as a place to hold retouching data. The beauty of this technique is that your original image is not altered in any way.

1   Open the Layers panel, and, if necessary, resize the panel so you can see all the elements. You should see the Web Layer, Layer 1, and Background layers. When you open a single image such as this one, Fireworks places the photo as an object on the Background layer, and also creates an empty layer called Layer 1.

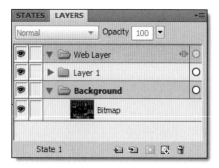

2   Select the photo in the Layers panel.

▶ **Tip:** Naming layers and objects helps you identify them as you work. Although not necessary, it's a good practice to follow.

3   Double-click the name Bitmap under the Background layer, and type **photo** to rename it.

4   Click the New Bitmap Image icon (⊞). A transparent (empty) Bitmap object will appear above the photo object.

Instant face-lift

Next, you will use the Rubber Stamp tool and the new bitmap object to take years off the actor's face.

1   Select the Zoom tool, and draw a selection around the actor's face.

2   Switch to the Rubber Stamp tool.

3   In the Properties panel, set Size to **5,** and leave Edge set to 100% for a nice subtle blend.

4 Select both the Source Aligned and Use Entire Document options.

When **Use Entire Document** is selected, Fireworks samples from all visible pixels on any layer or object in the design. When the option isn't selected, Fireworks samples only from the current object, which, as a new bitmap, has no actual pixels...yet.

5 Move the cursor above the top wrinkle at the left.

6 Hold down Alt (Windows) or Option (Mac) and click once to sample the skin tone above the wrinkle.

7 Move the cursor straight down until it is directly over the first wrinkle.

8 Hold down the mouse button, and begin painting carefully toward the right, following the entire wrinkle.

9 When you are happy with the result, repeat steps 5–8 to remove the second wrinkle.

10 Turn off the retouching (Bitmap) layer by clicking the eye icon beside the layer name. The wrinkles return. Turn the layer back on, and the wrinkles vanish.

You might also notice a blue rectangle appear on the canvas, surrounding the retouching work. This is how Fireworks indicates a selected object.

Rubber-stamping can take a bit of practice, which is another reason to perform the retouching on a separate object. If your results aren't as good as you would like, you can just delete the bitmap object by selecting it and then dragging it to the Layers panel trash can icon.

One other item of note: because you are adding additional objects to a photo, you will most likely want to save this file as a Fireworks PNG file in order to maintain the objects and their editability. In fact, if you press Ctrl+S (Windows) or Command+S (Mac) at this time, Fireworks displays a dialog box explaining the choices you have and the repercussions of each.

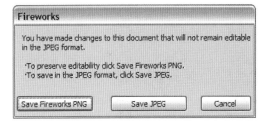

Layers *and* objects? Why?

Because the roots of Fireworks lie in the vector world—much like Adobe Illustrator—each layer can contain multiple objects. This concept may seem a little disconcerting if your experience is primarily with Photoshop, which is a layer-oriented application, but in fact, this *object-oriented* approach gives you much more control and flexibility over your designs. You can also create sublayers within a layer, which emulate the layer-groups workflow of Photoshop.

In the retouching workflow described in this chapter, you could just as easily have selected the empty Layer 1, added a bitmap object to that layer, and performed your rubber-stamping. It's really your choice.

Review questions

1   What is the maximum canvas size in Fireworks, and how can this affect your workflow?

2   What is the process for cropping a specific bitmap object in a design?

3   What options do you have for adjusting the tonal range of a bitmap image?

4   What are the advantages of Live Filters over traditional filters?

5   How do you use the Rubber Stamp tool, and what is a recommended workflow for using it?

Review answers

1   The maximum canvas size you can create in Fireworks is 6000 x 6000 pixels. If you have a very large file that you want to use in Fireworks, consider scaling it to more suitable dimensions before opening it in Fireworks.

2   Select the bitmap object, and then choose Edit > Crop Selected Bitmap. This will ensure that you're cropping only one object rather than the entire design.

3   If the entire image is too dark or too light, you can use the Levels dialog box to alter overall brightness and contrast. If you want to alter specific areas in the image, you can use the Dodge tool to lighten an area, or the Burn tool to darken an area.

4   Live Filters are nondestructive and completely editable at any time. Live Filters can also be applied to both vector and bitmap objects, whereas traditional filters can be applied only to bitmap objects.

5   The Rubber Stamp tool can be used only on bitmap objects, and is designed to copy pixels from one location to another, for the purpose of correcting defects or removing unwanted elements within a photo. You must first sample the area you want to use as a source by pressing Alt (Windows) or Option (Mac) and clicking on the desired area. Then you can move the cursor to the problem area and paint over it. Ideally, this type of retouching should be done within a new bitmap object, so you do not alter the original source image.

4 WORKING WITH SELECTIONS

Lesson overview

Making selections on a bitmap image is an important component of working with bitmaps. Bitmap selections isolate a specific area for alteration, protecting all other areas from being affected. For example, you might want to brighten a dark part of an image. Without a selection, this change in pixel brightness would be applied to the entire photo. In this lesson, you'll learn how to do the following:

- Make specific areas of an image active using selection tools

- Create a selection with the Magic Wand tool

- Adjust the edge of a bitmap selection

- Apply corrective filters to a selection

- Make complex selections using the Lasso and Magic Wand tools

- Modify a bitmap selection

- Save a bitmap selection for future use

- Deselect a selection

- Convert a bitmap selection to a path

 This lesson takes approximately 60 minutes to complete. Copy the Lesson04 folder into the Lessons folder that you created on your hard drive for these projects (or create it now, if you haven't already done so). As you work on this lesson, you won't preserve the start files. If you need to restore the start files, copy them from the *Adobe Fireworks CS5 Classroom in a Book* CD.

Making selections on a bitmap image is key to working with bitmaps regardless of the software application.

Understanding bitmap selections

The bitmap selection tools are helpful if you want to alter or copy a specific area of an image. Before you begin this lesson, though, you must also be clear on the difference between selecting an object and making a bitmap selection.

When you click on an object in the Layers panel, or use the Pointer tool to click on an object on the canvas, you are selecting (or activating) the entire object. You can then move, copy, edit, or cut that object from the design, without affecting anything else on the canvas. A bitmap selection differs in that you are selecting a specific part of a bitmap image rather than the entire bitmap object. Once you've made a selection, you can only copy or edit the area within the selection border.

Bitmap selection tools: a primer

The selection tools in Fireworks include the Marquee and Oval Marquee tools, the Lasso and Polygon Lasso tools, and the Magic Wand tool.

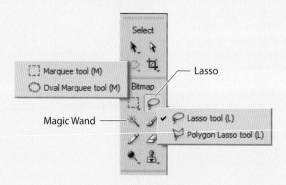

Choose the selection tool most suitable for the job. Use the Marquee (□) or Oval Marquee (◯) tool to select regularly shaped areas. Simply click and drag to draw out one of these selections after choosing the appropriate tool. Holding Shift constrains the rectangular marquee to a square and the oval marquee to a circle.

One of the Lasso tools (the standard Lasso ◌ or the Polygon Lasso ◌ tool) may be better suited to select irregular areas when you make a freehand selection. The standard Lasso Tool allows you to draw a selection on the canvas using a mouse or stylus. You outline the selection by clicking to plot points around the area you want selected. You can hold down Shift to constrain Polygon Lasso marquee segments to 45-degree increments. To close the polygon selection, either click the starting point or double-click in the workspace.

If the area is full of similar shades of colors, the Magic Wand tool (◌) may be your best choice to quickly create a selection. The Magic Wand tool selects pixels based on color. If you have an area of similarly colored pixels in your image (a blue sky, for example), the Magic Wand can quickly select that part of your image. You start the selection by clicking the wand cursor on an area of your image. The wand selects contiguous pixels of the same color range, based on the Tolerance setting in the Properties panel. You can increase the tool's sensitivity by changing the Tolerance setting to a higher value.

Options

Most of the bitmap selection tools have the option to set the selection edge to Hard, Anti-alias, or Feather. A Hard edge gives you a jagged, pixelated selection. Anti-alias blends the selection with the area outside the selection. Feather creates a softer, less accurate, blended edge selection. Unlike with the other two edge settings, you can apply a pixel value to Feather to increase the blend between the inside and outside of the selection.

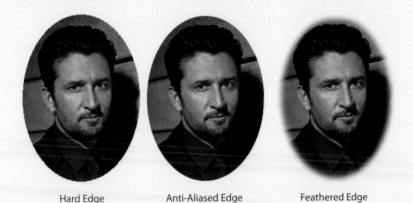

| Hard Edge | Anti-Aliased Edge | Feathered Edge |

Additional selection features for the marquee

If you choose the Rectangular or Elliptical Marquee, the Properties panel offers you additional options:

- Normal creates a marquee in which the height and width are independent of each other.
- Fixed Ratio constrains the height and width to defined ratios.
- Fixed Size sets the height and width to a defined dimension, in pixels.

Using Live Marquee

The Live Marquee feature is available for the bitmap selection tools listed earlier. By default, it is active (selected) in the Properties panel. Live Marquee gives you immediate control over the edge of your bitmap selection after it has been drawn. You can choose Hard for an aliased, hard-edged selection; Anti-alias for a softer, slightly blended selection edge; or Feather for a very soft blend. When you choose Feather, you set the amount of feathering you want. This amount will gradually blend any effect applied to the bitmap selection on both the inner and outer edges of the selection.

Getting started

Various images may require different types of adjustments. In this lesson, you will use a variety of selection tools to make local adjustments on three different images. You will start with a simple selection exercise using the Magic Wand.

1 Choose File > Open, and browse to the Lesson04 folder.

2 Select Backdrop02.jpg, and then click Open.

   Notice how bright the sky is—practically without detail. You will apply a bitmap filter to a bitmap selection, which will permanently change the pixels in the image. When you are going to apply permanent changes to a bitmap object, it's a good idea to create a duplicate of the image first so that the original is not damaged.

3 Select the Pointer tool, and click on the image to make it active.

4 Press Ctrl+Shift+D (Windows) or Command+Shift+D (Mac) to create a clone of the image. You now have two bitmap images in the Layers panel.

5 In the Layers panel, double-click the bottom bitmap image name, and change it to **Original**.

6 Double-click the top image, and rename it **Retouching**.

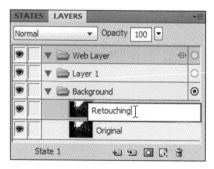

Selecting and modifying with the Magic Wand tool

In this section, you are going to use the Magic Wand tool to select a part of the scene in order to apply an exposure adjustment.

Creating the selection

First, create the selection using the Magic Wand tool.

1 Select the Magic Wand tool (⬚) from the Tools panel.

2 Move the cursor over the sky portion of the image, and click once. As illustrated here, a selection appears.

3 To see how our alteration blends with the rest of the photo, choose View > Edges (or press Ctrl+H on Windows or Option+F9 on Mac). This hides the selection from view but still lets you perform actions on it, such as applying filters.

4 Choose Filters > Adjust Color > Levels.

5 Set the Shadow (Minimum Intensity) value to **20**.

6 Set the Midtone (Gamma) value to **0.4**, and leave the Highlight value at 255. You can do this by typing into the input boxes or dragging the middle sliders.

7 Toggle Preview off and on again repeatedly to see how the cloud definition has changed, and then click OK to apply the filter.

● **Note:** When applying a filter adjustment to a bitmap selection, you must use the main Filters menu. You should also create a copy of the image before you begin.

▶ **Tip:** It's a good idea to zoom in on the area you are selecting to ensure a more accurate selection.

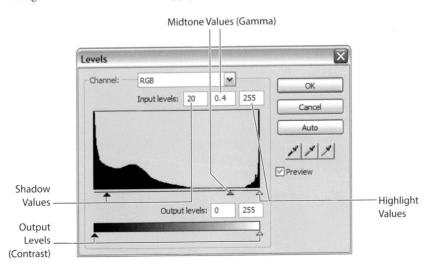

8 Close the file without saving.

Using the Magic Wand tool with keyboard modifiers

Because the Magic Wand tool selects based on contiguous pixel color, areas you want included may not always become part of your original selection. You can use modifier keys to add to the selection.

In this exercise, you are going to use the Magic Wand tool to select parts of the actors' faces in order to apply an exposure adjustment. You will also modify the selection by applying a feathered edge.

1   Choose File > Open, and browse to the Lesson04 folder.

2   Select actors_together.jpg, and then click Open.

Notice the skin tones on the left cheek of the man. They're almost washed out. A similar problem exists with the woman's face. You will be applying a bitmap filter to a bitmap selection, which will permanently change the pixels in the image. When you are going to apply permanent changes to a bitmap object, you should create a duplicate of the image first so that the original is not damaged.

3   Select the Pointer tool, and click the image to make it active.

4   Press Ctrl+Shift+D (Windows) or Command+Shift+D (Mac) to create a clone of the image, and rename this duplicate **Retouching**.

5   If necessary, select the Magic Wand tool () from the Tools panel.

6   In the Properties panel, set the Edge to Feather, input a value of **4**, set the Tolerance to **32**, and make sure the Live Marquee option is selected.

7   Move the cursor to the bright area of the detective's cheek, and click once. A selection appears.

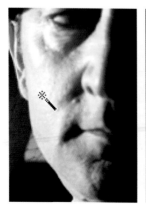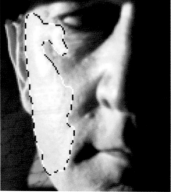

Notice that the other bright areas on the woman (her cheek and nose) are not part of the selection. This is because these areas are separated by pixels that are much darker and of different colors, and not within the Tolerance setting of the tool. Increasing the tolerance is not the answer, either, because we would end up selecting more areas than we want for this adjustment.

8 Hold down the Shift key, and click on the bright part of the woman's cheek, between her ear and her eye.

9 Hold down the Shift key one more time, and click on the bright side of the bridge of her nose. You now have three separate selections.

10 Choose Filters > Repeat Levels. (This option is available for the last filter applied, as long as you have not restarted Fireworks.)

11 Set the Gamma slider to a value of **0.6**.

Note: To subtract from a selection, hold down the Alt (Windows) or Option (Mac) keys. These modifiers work with the Rubber Stamp, Lasso, Marquee, and Oval Marquee tools.

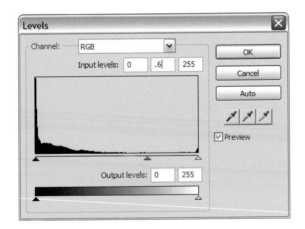

12 Click OK to apply the filter. You'll see that the skin tones of the actors' faces look much more even and are no longer washed out.

If you create a particularly complex selection, such as the one you've just done, you might want to save your efforts as an alpha channel in order to reuse the selection at a later time. See the sidebar "Saving and restoring bitmap selections." (Your file is currently in the perfect position to use these bitmap-selection functions.)

Finally, it's time to finish up with this file.

13 Choose File > Save.

Fireworks recognizes that this altered image has properties that are not supported in a flat JPEG file, so you will see a dialog box asking you for a decision about which type of file you'd like to save. If you want to retain the editability of the file, save it as a Fireworks PNG file. If the original image and the bitmap selection are not important, you can opt to save the file as a flat JPEG.

▶ **Tip:** Sometimes the marquee itself can get in your way. You can quickly show or hide the marquee by pressing Ctrl+H (Windows) or Option+F9 (Mac).

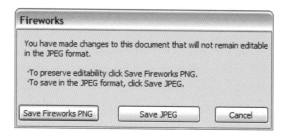

14 Click Save Fireworks PNG. This will maintain the selection information and both bitmap images. The Save dialog box appears.

15 Name the file **actors_together_retouched.png**, save it to the Lesson04 folder, and click OK.

● **Note:** If you had chosen File > Save As, Fireworks would assume you want to save the file as a JPEG. There's a warning message in the Save As dialog box; pay attention to it! Some people don't notice the warning and later reopen their file only to learn the edits have been flattened, and the original unaltered image has been lost. Make sure you click on the Save As Type options and choose the format you prefer.

Saving and restoring bitmap selections

Once you've created a complex selection, you can save it, giving you the option to deselect it, work on other parts of the image, and come back to that selection later. These functions are available regardless of the selection tool you've used in the first place. To save a selection, you first need to have an active bitmap selection.

1   Choose Select > Save Bitmap Selection.

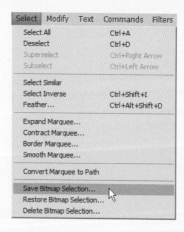

2 In the Save Selection dialog box, change the name to **cheek**. Leave all other settings as they are.

3 Click OK.

Once a selection is saved, you can then call it up any time you need it during your session. If you save the file as a Fireworks PNG file, the selection remains with the file and can be restored even after the file has been closed and reopened.

Note: If you have more than one saved selection, you can choose the correct one from the Selection menu in the Restore Selection dialog box. In the current exercise, the "cheek" selection is the only one in the list.

4 Press Ctrl+D (Windows) or Command+Shift+A (Mac) to deselect the bitmap selections on the canvas (so that you can see how to restore it).

5 Choose Select > Restore Bitmap Selection.

6 Click OK. The selection reappears on the canvas.

Selecting with the lasso tools

Selection tools are also interchangeable; you might start with the Magic Wand tool, for example, but then turn to the Lasso tool ( ) to refine a selection.

1 Choose File > Open, and browse to the Lesson04 folder.

2 Open the file called Mark_actor07.jpg.

3 Select the Magic Wand tool once again.

4 Set Edge to Anti-alias, its value to **0**, and Tolerance to **32**, and make sure the Live Marquee option is selected.

5 Click on the gray cinderblock wall.

● **Note:** If you don't see the selection appear, make sure that the marquee is not hidden by selecting View > Edges.

6 Hold down the Shift key, and click on other areas of the wall. Avoid clicking the shadow of the detective, because this will also select parts of the gun.

7 Continuing to press the Shift key, click the dark segment to the right of the actor.

8 Select the Lasso tool.

9 Holding down the Shift key, draw around a large part of the shadow. Avoid lassoing the gun. You do not have to do this in one operation; indeed, it's a good idea to zoom in for the more detailed areas and add to the selection in multiple steps.

As long as you hold down the Shift key, you can add to the existing selection. If you select an area by accident, you can switch to the Alt (Windows) or Option (Mac) key and draw around the unwanted area.

When you are done, everything except the detective should be selected.

Note: Creating this selection took some time, so it's wise to save the selection as you did with the previous document (choose Select > Save Bitmap Selection).

10 Choose File > Save.

11 Click Save Fireworks PNG.

The Save As dialog box appears.

12 Name the file **Mark_actor07.fw.png**. Because you are using a different file type, you can still keep the same filename.

13 Save the file to the Lesson04 folder and click OK.

Converting a selection to a path

In Fireworks, you can easily convert bitmap selections to vector paths. Paths can be easier to edit than bitmap selections, in part because you aren't as likely to delete an entire path by accident. If you are adjusting a bitmap selection and forget to use the Shift and Alt (Windows) or Option (Mac) modifier keys, you can easily delete the entire selection. To edit the shape of a path, you can use the Subselection tool ( ) to drag individual control points in the path.

In this exercise, you will continue working with the Mark_actor07.fw.png file.

1 If the selection is not active, choose Select > Restore Bitmap Selection.

2 Choose Select > Convert Marquee To Path.

The selection is removed, and in its place is a new path object, filled with the last attributes used for vector objects.

3 Select the Pointer tool, if it's not already selected.

4 Choose Pattern > Wood 3 from the Fill Category list in the Properties panel.

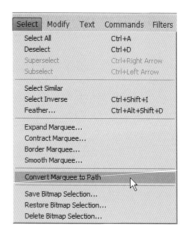

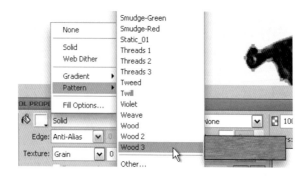

The detective is now up against another type of wall, so to speak. In the Layers panel, the newly created vector object is called a composite path.

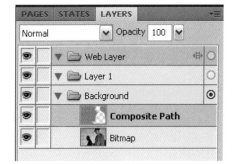

5 Double-click the object name in the Layers panel and change it to **wall**.

6 Rename the bitmap image **detective**.

7 Choose File > Save.

You will learn much more about working with paths in Lesson 4.

Other selection options

Select Inverse

Sometimes, selecting the unwanted part of the image is easier.

The Select Inverse command toggles between the active selection and the unselected area.

Let's say you have a photo of a city scene with a clear sky in the background. You want to do some levels or filter adjustments to the city area. Using the Magic Wand tool to select the evenly colored sky will be easier (and faster). Then you can choose Select > Select Inverse to reverse the selected areas, making the city scene the active selection.

Select Similar

Select Similar adds to the current bitmap selection, based on colors within the active selection. Anywhere the colors within the selection appear throughout the image, they will become part of the new selection. You can choose Select > Select Similar with any bitmap selection.

Modifying a selection

You can expand, contract, or smooth any active bitmap selection by choosing the desired action from the Select menu.

Review questions

1 What is the difference between selecting objects and making bitmap selections?

2 What are the five bitmap selection tools in Fireworks, and what are their functions?

3 What does the Tolerance setting do when you're using the Magic Wand tool?

4 What are the two keyboard modifiers you can use in conjunction with the bitmap selection tools?

5 How do you create a clone of a bitmap image? Why would you do this?

Review answers

1 When you click on an object in the Layers panel or use the Pointer tool to click an object on the canvas, you are selecting (or activating) the entire object, allowing you to move, copy, edit, or cut that object from the design, without affecting anything else on the canvas. A bitmap selection differs from this in that you are selecting a specific part of a bitmap image rather than the entire object. Once you've made a selection, you can copy or edit only the area within the selection border. The bitmap selection tools cannot be used on vector objects.

2 The Fireworks selection tools are the Marquee and Oval Marquee tools, the Lasso and Polygon Lasso tools, and, finally, the Magic Wand tool.

   Typically, you use the Marquee or Oval Marquee tool to select regularly shaped areas, and the Lasso or Polygon Lasso tool to select irregular areas. You use the Magic Wand tool to select pixels based on color. While drawing the initial selection, the Shift key constrains the marquee tools to symmetrical objects (squares and circles) and the Polygon Lasso tool segments to 45-degree increments.

   After a selection has been created, hold down the Shift Key to add to the selection. Pressing Alt (Windows) or Option (Mac) subtracts from a selection.

3 The Magic Wand tool selects contiguous pixels of the same color range based on the tolerance setting in the Properties panel. You can increase the tool's sensitivity by changing the Tolerance setting in the Properties panel to a higher value.

4 The Shift key is one of the keyboard modifiers you can use with bitmap selection tools, and the Alt (Windows) or Option (Mac) key is the other. Both of these modifiers work with the Rubber Stamp and freehand Lasso tools, as well as the rectangular and elliptical marquees. Holding down the Shift key lets you add to an existing selection. To subtract from a selection, hold down Alt (Windows) or Option (Mac).

5 To clone a bitmap image (or any other object), press Ctrl+Shift+D (Windows) or Command+Shift+D (Mac), or choose Edit > Clone to create a clone of the image. Creating a clone of your original image lets you edit and retouch a copy without damaging the original.

5 WORKING WITH VECTOR GRAPHICS

Lesson overview

Using vector tools is intuitive, but to the new user, these tools may seem a bit intimidating. In Fireworks (similar to Illustrator or Flash), you can draw almost any shape at all by using vectors. Now is your chance to familiarize yourself with several vector tools, including vector shapes and the Pen tool. You will also use the Properties panel and Subselection tool to modify vectors you've created. In this lesson, you'll learn how to do the following:

- Draw simple vector shapes
- Use guides to place objects on the canvas
- Identify the differences between vector and bitmap images
- Use the 9-Slice Scaling tool to scale vector shapes
- Use Auto Shapes
- Create paths with the Pen tool
- Edit paths with the Pen and Subselection tools
- Create a custom shape
- Customize the fill and stroke of a vector shape

 This lesson takes approximately 90 minutes to complete. Copy the Lesson05 folder into the Lessons folder that you created on your hard drive for these projects (or create it now, if you haven't already done so). As you work on this lesson, you won't preserve the start files. If you need to restore the start files, copy them from the *Adobe Fireworks CS5 Classroom in a Book* CD.

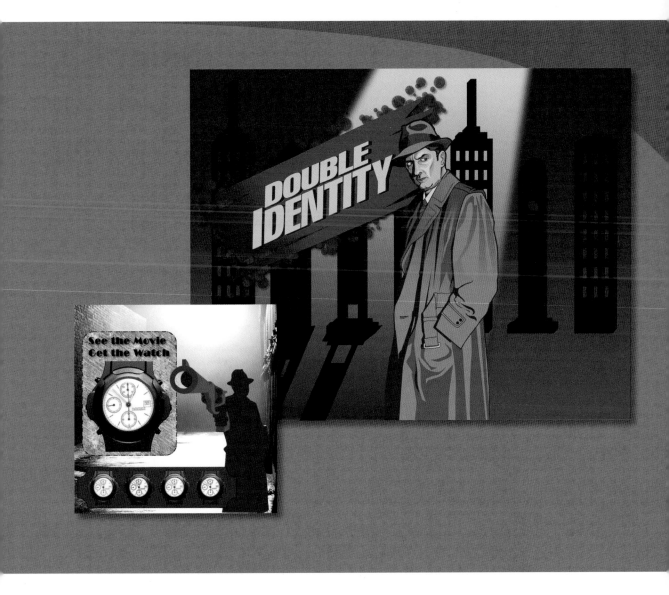

Vectors are a powerful component of Fireworks,
giving you the flexibility to create unique custom
shapes or call on the many prebuilt vectors that
are part of Fireworks.

About vectors

Note: Most designs contain elements to hold other objects such as text and graphics, and when standard shapes aren't enough, you can turn to the Pen tool to create your own custom vector shapes or paths.

Computer drawings that use mathematical equations to draw lines and fills onscreen are known as *vectors*. A vector is simply the path between two defined points on the screen, with properties such as color and thickness applied to the path.

Fireworks comes with a range of prebuilt vector shapes, most of which are found in the Tools panel in their very own section. There is also a series of special prebuilt Auto Shapes that can be found in the Shapes panel.

The most commonly used vector tools are the Text, Shape, and Pen tools.

Basic vector drawing techniques

The Tools panel contains several basic vector shapes, which include the Line tool, the Rectangle tool, the Ellipse tool, and the Polygon tool. (You've already worked with the Rectangle and Ellipse tools in Lesson 1.) To create one of these shapes, select the appropriate tool, and then click and drag on the canvas. These basic shapes can be scaled, skewed, and distorted using the Transform tools in the Tools panel. You can use the Properties panel to change the fill and stroke and even add a texture for a more realistic look.

Note: Text is also a vector, but you're focusing on shapes and paths in this lesson.

With a bit of practice, you'll be creating your own custom vector shapes and masks before you know it. But we'll start off simply by adding a couple of vector shapes to the watch_promo.fw.png file you worked with in Lessons 1 and 2, and then altering those shapes and learning how to use guides for more precise placement.

Deleting shapes

In Lesson 1, you created an ellipse. In Lesson 3, you hid and locked it. Now you'll delete it.

1 Choose File > Open, and navigate to the Lesson05 folder.

2 Select the watch_promo.fw.png file, and click Open.

3 Click the lock icon next to the ellipse in the Layers panel to unlock the object.

4 If it's not already selected, select the ellipse in the Layers panel.

5 Drag the layer to the Delete Selection (trash can) icon in the Layers panel.

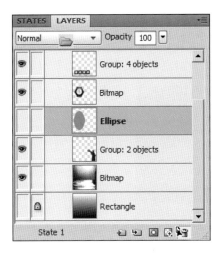

Adding guides

Guides are great tools for aligning and placing objects on the canvas. To help place the new shape, you will set up guides on the canvas.

1 If rulers are not already visible, choose View > Rulers.

2 Move your cursor over the left ruler.

3 Click and drag toward the canvas. You will see a vertical guide appear. You will also see a tooltip appear beside the guide, with an x value. This value is the horizontal position of the vertical guide, as measured in pixels.

4 When the tooltip displays x:19, let go of the mouse. The guide drops at that location.

5 Drag another vertical guide, and place it at 255 pixels.

6 Drag guides from the top ruler to these positions: 125 pixels and 362 pixels. If you need to reposition guides, you can simply select them with the Pointer tool and drag them to a new position.

Note: Tooltips are visible only if View > Tooltips is selected.

Tip: If you want a higher degree of accuracy, double-click on the guide and then set the location numerically.

Tip: To quickly toggle grids on or off, use keyboard shortcuts: Command+; (Mac) or Ctrl+; (Windows)

Measuring distances between guides

Once guides are drawn, you can easily measure the distance between guides.

1 Select the Pointer tool and then place your cursor over the watch.

2 Hold down the Shift key. Note the distances that appear along with dashed lines and arrowheads (the areas highlighted in red in the following figure). These are guide measurements, and they can be invoked any time you have guides on the canvas. The guide dimensions should be 236 x 237 pixels.

3   Move the cursor around the canvas. The guide measurements will update based on the nearest guides.

Placing an object using guides

Once guides have been placed, you can accurately draw the new shape, as long as objects are set to snap to guides.

1   Choose View > Guides, and make sure that Snap To Guides is selected.

2   Select the Rectangle tool from the Tools panel.

3   Move the cursor onto the canvas, near the upper-left intersection of the guides that box in the large watch. Click and drag to draw a rectangle. When you come within 5 pixels of the guides on the right and bottom, the rectangle snaps to those guides, giving you an exact dimension, placed exactly where you want it to be.

4   Before releasing the mouse, press the Up Arrow key four times. If you pay close attention to the rectangle you are drawing, you will see the corners become rounded.

5   Release the mouse. The shape appears, with all of the Fill properties that were used last. It will also cover the watch.

6 In the Properties panel, set the Fill Category to Solid and the color to medium gray (#999999).

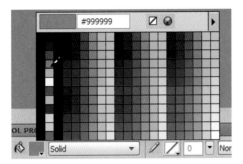

7 If necessary, expand the Layers panel so that you can see both the new rectangle and the watch layers.

8 Double-click the new rectangle name, and change it to **watch background**.

9 Drag the watch background object below the watch in the Layers panel to change the stacking order.

Resizing vectors

Early in the creation of the watch_promo.fw.png file, you added a grouped vector shape in the form of a silhouetted detective pointing a rather exaggerated gun. You are going to resize this vector object, with the added side benefit of seeing how this resizing affects—or doesn't affect—the quality of a vector.

1 Select the detective silhouette using the Pointer tool.

2 Select the Scale tool, and drag the object inward from any corner to make it proportionately smaller.

3 Press Enter or Return to accept the new size. Note that other than the reduced size, the object does not appear damaged or altered. The edges and overall shape have not been distorted.

4 Select the Scale tool again.

5 Drag the upper-left corner of the scale handles up and to the left, until the tooltips read approximately w:250, h:369.

If you had treated a bitmap image in this manner (sizing down, and then sizing up beyond the original size), the image quality of the bitmap would have decreased noticeably. The edges could become jagged and the image itself would become pixelated. This vector shape, however, remains undamaged.

Changing the appearance of basic vector shapes

As mentioned earlier, you can scale, skew, and distort basic vector shapes using the Transform tools in the Tools panel (hidden under the Scale tool). You can change their fill, stroke, color, and even texture using the Properties panel. In this section we'll concentrate on basic modifications.

1 Select the gray rectangle you created in the previous exercise.

2 In the Properties panel, choose Pattern > Paint Blue from the Fill Category menu.

3 Below the Fill Category menu, choose Onyx from the Texture menu.

4 Adjust the amount of the texture to **40%**.

5 Still in the Properties panel, from the Stroke Category menu, choose Dashed > Dash Double.

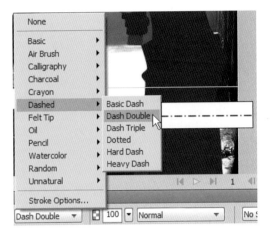

6 Set the stroke color to Black from the color picker in the Stroke section.

7 Set the Tip Size to a value of **2**. The end result should be similar to what you see below.

8 In the Layers panel, make sure the detective object is stacked above the rounded rectangle. This creates a sense of depth in the design, as the detective object now slightly overlaps the rectangle.

Feel free to try other textures and strokes. If the stroke is heavy enough, you can even add a texture to it to further enhance the effect.

Bitmap and vector graphics: What's the difference?

The intrinsic ability of Fireworks to move back and forth between vectors and bitmaps—and even combine both graphic types—makes it a powerful creative tool. But it's important to understand the differences between these two types of graphics, so you can know which to use in any situation.

As the name implies, bitmap graphics (also referred to as "raster") are made of a specific number of pixels "mapped" to a grid. Each pixel has a specific location and color value. The greater the number of pixels, the higher the resolution of the image and the larger the file size. If you resize a bitmap image, you are either adding to or taking away pixels from the image, and this will affect image quality and file size. The initial number of pixels in a bitmap image is set at the time of capture (when taking a digital photo or scanning an image, for example).

Vector graphics are, simply put, mathematical equations describing the distance and angle between two points. Additional information, such as the color and thickness of the line (stroke) and the contents of the path (fill), can also be set. Unlike bitmap graphics, vectors can be resized up or down with no detrimental impact to the vector shape itself.

Another example of the differences between vector and bitmap is this: A photograph can accurately depict a physical scene in a single image layer. Producing similar realism in a vector illustration could require hundreds and hundreds of vector shapes stacked on each other.

This is not to suggest that bitmaps are better than vectors, or vice versa; both of these main graphic types are integral to visual communication.

Scaling vector objects

In Lesson 2, we talked about how scaling—whether for bitmap or vector shapes—can cause unwanted distortion, and how the 9-slice Scaling tool eliminates that problem. Because this is such a useful tool, and because it's a bit different for vectors, we'll practice with it again, this time scaling the rounded rectangle in the watch_promo.fw.png file to make it large enough to hold the text that you will be adding to the design.

Scaling the "old" way

Remember, traditional scaling will distort the corner radii of this rectangle, giving you an undesirable result. Let's try this first to see what happens.

1   Make sure the rectangle is still active; look for the blue control handles at the four corners of the shape. If you don't see them, use the Pointer tool to select the shape on the canvas or in the Layers panel.

2   Select the Scale tool ( ) from the Select section in the Tools panel. Control handles appear around the rectangle.

3   Drag the top-middle control handle straight up by 60 pixels. Refer to the tooltips as you drag the handle.

4   Release the mouse, and note how the corners of the rectangle have been distorted. (If the guides or the rectangle's bounding box are obscuring your view of the corners, click Preview on the Document window, but be sure to click back to Original to continue working.)

5   Press the Esc key to cancel the transformation, or press Ctrl+Z (Windows) or Command+Z (Mac) to undo the scaling if the rectangle is no longer active or if another tool was selected.

Distortion-free vector scaling with the 9-slice Scaling tool

Now let's see how big of an improvement we get with this method.

1   Drag in a guide from the top ruler, and position it at 64 pixels. (Tooltips do not display when using the 9-slice Scaling tool, so this step is necessary in order to set an accurate height.)

2   Select the 9-Slice Scaling tool from the Tools panel. As in the previous exercise, the scaling handles appear again, but the image is now divided with special 9-slice guides. The default settings are fine in this case.

Note: The 9-slice guides can be repositioned prior to the scaling operation; any elements in the four corners created by the guides do not scale.

3 Drag the top-middle control handle straight up to the guide. Note that the corners do not distort this time.

4 Double-click inside the object or press Enter or Return to accept the new dimensions.

Adding text to your design

Images and text go together in many designs. In this exercise, you will add a call-to-action tagline to the design.

1 Select the Text tool.

2 In the Properties panel, choose a showy, bold font family (we chose Cooper Std).

3 Set a large font size. For Cooper Std we chose 24 points; if you are using another font, start at 24 and see if that size works for you.

4 Set Fill Color to Black.

Text engine integration

Since CS4, Fireworks uses the same text engine as Illustrator and Photoshop, so copying and pasting text from these applications, or opening a Photoshop file containing text, has become much more predictable. Prior to CS4, Fireworks used its own proprietary type engine to render fonts. If you open a Fireworks CS3 or earlier source PNG file, Fireworks CS4 prompts you to update the fonts in the file. In most cases, updating the fonts is recommended, but you may have to reposition your text areas once the update has been completed.

5 Type **See the Movie**.

6 Press Enter or Return, and then type **Get the Watch**.

If you find the spacing between your letters is too narrow, you can set the tracking to a higher value. Tracking adjusts the space between two adjacent characters, and is the method Fireworks uses for manual kerning (spacing) of letters.

7 Use the Pointer tool to select the text box.

8 Change the tracking value to alter the distance between letters. Using the Cooper Std font, we adjusted the tracking to a value of 40.

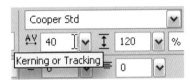

9 Set the font's weight to bold. If the font has multiple families, you can do this in the Font Style menu in the Properties panel. If the font doesn't have any derivatives, you can apply faux bold by clicking the B icon.

10 Use the Pointer tool to position the text area so it is centered left to right within the rectangle. A Smart Guide appears when you're in the correct location.

To dress up the text a bit more, you can add a Live Filter.

11 In the Filters area of the Properties panel, click the Add Live Filter button, and then choose Shadow And Glow > Drop Shadow. Set the Distance to 4, and click away from the Live Filter settings to close them.

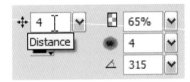

▶ **Tip:** If you find the guides getting in the way, you can hide them temporarily by pressing Ctrl+; (Windows) or Command+; (Mac), or by choosing View > Guides > Show Guides. You can clear the guides completely by choosing View > Guides > Clear Guides.

Note: You will learn more about working with text in Lesson 7.

Working with Auto Shapes

Auto Shapes are art with JavaScript logic attached. They include additional diamond-shaped control points that let you alter visual properties, such as corner roundness, corner shape, or the number of points in a star. Most of these control points also have tooltips that describe how they affect the Auto Shape. You will now add an Auto Shape as a background for the watch thumbnails.

1 Choose the Chamfer Rectangle tool from the Vector section of the Tools panel (click and hold the Rectangle tool to see the other tools available).

2 Drag out the shape so it covers the width and height of the four watch thumbnails. When you release the mouse, you'll see the yellow diamonds in each corner. You'll also see that the shape takes on the properties of the last vector shape, which can make for a pretty busy-looking design.

3 If necessary, change the Fill setting from Pattern to Solid.

4 Set the fill color to **#343434**, matching the gray background of the watches.

5 Make sure the Stroke category is set to None.

6 Click on one of the four yellow corner diamonds to toggle the corners of your shape to other designs. Keep clicking until the chamfer shape returns.

7 Resize the total shape by clicking and dragging the fifth yellow diamond, located near the bottom right of the shape. Set the dimensions to 390 pixels wide by 100 pixels high.

8 In the Layers panel, rename the new shape **sample background** and adjust the stacking order so that the sample background is below the watches.

9 Use the Pointer tool to reposition the shape so it is centered under the watch group. Smart Guides will help you align the objects. Toggle the shape's visibility off if needed.

10 From the Stroke Category menu, choose Pencil > 1-Pixel Soft and set the stroke color to black (#000000). Your final design should be similar to this.

▶ **Tip:** The Auto Shapes panel (Window > Auto Shapes) contains a collection of even more complex shapes. You can download other shapes from the Adobe Exchange at www.adobe.com/ cfusion/exchange/. You will have to sign up first, but membership is free.

11 Save and close the file.

Understanding paths and the Pen tool

The Pen tool lets you create custom shapes and paths by drawing with the mouse or a stylus. You can also use it to edit existing shapes by adding anchor points. Unlike the Pencil bitmap tool, where you basically just click and drag to draw a bitmap line, using the Pen tool involves clicking the mouse to set a straight line between two anchor points (a place where the path can change direction) or clicking and dragging to create a curved section of a path. Every time you want to change the direction of a path, you move the mouse to the desired position and then click to set an anchor point.

Let's try out the Pen tool in a new document.

1   Create a new document that is 500 x 500 pixels.

2   Set the Canvas color to white if it isn't already, and click OK.

3   Select the Pen tool.

4   Make sure a stroke color has been applied, so you'll be able to see and select the finished path later. Black is fine.

5   Click once near the left side of the canvas.

6   Move your mouse near the middle of the canvas.

7   Click again to set another anchor point.

8   Move the mouse to the right area of the canvas.

9   This time, instead of just clicking the mouse, hold down the mouse button and *drag*. This will pull out curve control arms for that section of the path.

10 When you have drawn a curve to your satisfaction, release the mouse button. As you add more anchor points, Fireworks displays the path outline in blue.

If you move the mouse around, you will see the Pen tool is still active. To disengage the tool, do one of the following:

•   Close the path (create a shape) by clicking the original starting anchor point.

•   Double-click the last anchor point to create an open path.

Anchor point basics

Anchor points have two states: straight and curved. You can convert a straight point to a curved point by using the Pen tool to click and drag out the curve control arms, also known as Bezier control arms.

To convert a curved anchor to a straight point, just click on it once with the Pen tool. Click a second time to delete the anchor point entirely.

If you want to delete a straight anchor point, select it with the Subselection tool, and press the Delete key.

Other vector tools

Vector Path tool

The Vector Path tool ( ) can be handy if you like to draw vector shapes in a more freehand manner. While it's best suited for a stylus, due to the precise control and varying degrees of pressure that a tablet allows, you can also use a mouse to draw independent paths.

Redraw Path tool

The Redraw Path tool ( ) gives you another way to edit a vector shape or path without having to use the Pen tool. Much like the Vector Path tool, you use this freehand, to draw a new path and connect it to an existing path to change its shape. Draw outside the existing path to add to the shape or draw inside to cut away from the shape. The path's stroke, fill, and effects are retained.

Freeform tool

The Freeform tool ( ) lets you bend and reshape vectors interactively instead of altering anchor points. You use this tool to push or pull any part of a path, and Fireworks adds, moves, or deletes points along the path as you change the vector object's shape.

Reshape Area tool

The Reshape Area tool ( ) is another way to distort a path. It pulls the area of all selected paths within the outer circle of the reshape-area pointer. Think of it as a smudge tool for vectors, but instead of smearing pixels, it alters a path's shape.

Path Scrubber

The Path Scrubbers (,) are interesting tools. They don't change the path; rather, you use them to alter the heaviness of the stroke which is applied to the path. They affect the stroke only in the areas you paint over with the tool. This can give the stroke a bit more of a hand-drawn look.

Editing paths

Creating paths and shapes is empowering (and fun!), but it's only half the battle. Knowing how to edit vectors—that is, to be able to customize them—is equally important.

Adding points with the Pen tool

You can add anchor points to an existing path using the Pen tool. You will do this with the path from the previous exercise.

1   Make sure the path is active by selecting it with the Pointer tool.

2   Select the Pen tool.

3   Click on the path where you want the new anchor point to be; note the plus sign (+) that appears next to the Pen tool's cursor. Click once to add a straight path connection; click and drag to create a curved path section.

Note: If you add a point to a curved segment, it is automatically a curved anchor point.

4   To stop the Pen tool from adding to the end of an open path like this one, double-click the last control point in the path.

Note: If you see a crosshair cursor icon instead of the Pen icon, you will need to deselect the Precise Cursors option in the Edit area of the Preferences dialog box.

Editing paths with the Subselection tool

After a path is created, you can use the Subselection tool (⬚) to select and alter the location of individual anchor points, thus changing the shape of the path. The Subselection tool works similarly to the Direct Selection tool in Photoshop or Illustrator.

1   Select the Subselection tool from the Tools panel.

2   Move the tool to the middle anchor point of the path you created earlier. If the vector is no longer active (highlighted in blue), click anywhere on the path to activate it.

3   Click and drag the middle anchor point lower on the canvas. The path redraws when you release the mouse.

Note: To use the Subselection tool on Auto Shapes or on vectors created by the Rectangle tool, you must first ungroup them (choose Modify > Ungroup, or press Ctrl+Shift+G [Windows] or Command+Shift+G [Mac]). They will lose their unique characteristics: Auto Shapes will lose their yellow control handles, and you will no longer be able to change the corner radius of a rectangle from within the Properties panel.

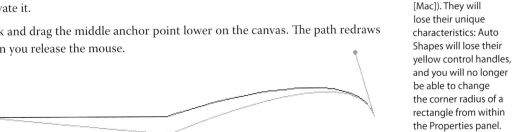

Creating custom shapes

Creating custom vector shapes opens up a lot of creative options. In this exercise, you will use the Pen tool to draw a custom vector shape. The file you will work on (street_scene.fw.png) is all vector artwork, from simple shapes in the background to complex vector illustration of the movie's lead actor. To practice custom shapes and other techniques, you'll be updating this file to look like street_scene_complete.fw.png.

To begin, you will create a stylized background to run behind the movie title in this design.

Drawing the shape

You will do your best to imitate the shape shown in the following figure. It's made up of a series of straight anchor point segments. This is a custom shape, so don't worry if you don't create an exact match. To help you further, you can make the original shape visible in the Layers panel and use it as a guide.

1   Open the street_scene.fw.png file from the Lesson05 folder.

2   Hide the detective object by clicking on its eye icon in the Layers panel. This will make it easier for you to trace the original shape. You can hide the skyline layer as well, if it is distracting you.

3   Select the Pen tool and specify the layer you'll draw on.

4   In the Properties panel, set Fill to None. For Stroke, choose Basic > Hard Line. Then set the stroke's color to **#990000** and Texture to **0%**.

5   Click and release the mouse to set each point for the shape. There is no need to click and drag any of these points as you set them, because they all need to be straight lines.

6 When you bring the cursor back to your starting point, notice that the Pen tool icon changes to the Pen tool with a small circle, indicating you can close the path by clicking. This closed path is your custom shape.

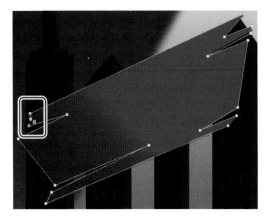

7 Select the Subselection tool.

8 If necessary, you can reposition any anchor points in the new object; use the mouse to reposition anchor points. Note how both paths extending from the anchor point adjust based on the new location of the anchor point. Feel free to adjust anchor points until you have the shape you want.

9 If you were using the original image as a guide, hide it now in the Layers panel.

10 Save the file.

Customizing fills and strokes

Creating a custom shape is just the beginning; once you have a vector object on the canvas, you can apply a variety of fill and stroke effects to it as well. Here, you're going to customize the look of your newly created custom shape by adding a gradient and a stylized stroke effect.

Adding a gradient fill

First you'll add the gradient, rotating it to match the original object.

1 If necessary, select the custom object you just created from the Layers panel. (Because this object has no fill, it's easier to select it from the Layers panel.)

2 Choose Gradient > Linear from the Fill Category menu in the Properties panel. A standard linear gradient appears.

3 Select the Pointer tool. A black control arm appears.

This "arm" controls the location, direction, angle, and length of the gradient fill. The arm has a circle control point at one end and a square control point at the other. The circle controls the position/starting point for the gradient; the square controls the angle and length. By default, the linear gradient runs from top to bottom, the full height of the object.

4 Use the mouse to click and drag the circle point so it rests on the top edge of the shape. As you drag, the gradient updates live on the canvas.

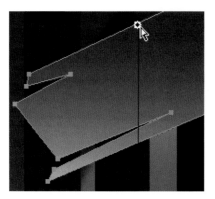

5 Move the mouse onto the arm itself. A rotation icon appears. Click and drag the arm so that it is roughly parallel to the angle of the shape.

6 Drag the circle point again so it is positioned in the gap of the shape at the lower left.

7 Drag the square control point to shorten the gradient and to change its angle.

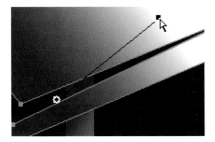

8 Click the Fill Color box. The Edit Gradient pop-up window opens.

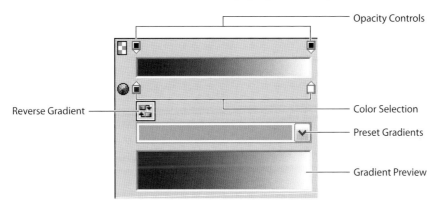

Opacity Controls

Reverse Gradient

Color Selection

Preset Gradients

Gradient Preview

9 Click the left color swatch, and when the color picker appears, type **#252A41** in the input field. Then press Enter or Return.

10 Click the right color swatch, input **#C3112E**, and press Enter or Return.

11 To make the gradient smoother, select the Dither Gradient button () in the Properties panel.

12 Still within the Properties panel, click the Add Live Filters button, and choose Shadow And Glow > Drop Shadow to add a drop shadow to the object.

Customizing the stroke

Much like adding a fill to a vector, styling the stroke can also add impact and interest to an object. The plain red stroke we've got currently is okay, but to achieve a sense of grittiness and danger, you will customize the stroke using one of the preset Stroke categories.

1 Making sure the object is still selected, set the Tip Size to **38**.

2 From the Stroke menu, choose Oil > Splatter.

3 Choose Stroke Options from the Stroke menu.

None

Basic
Air Brush
Calligraphy
Charcoal
Crayon
Dashed
Felt Tip
Oil
Pencil
Watercolor
Random
Unnatural

Stroke Options...

Splatter

4 Select the Fill Over Stroke option, and click away from the Stroke Options panel to close it. This hides the stroke effect inside the shape.

5 Change the stroke's edge softness to **19**.

6 Choose DNA from the Texture menu, and set the value to **30%**.

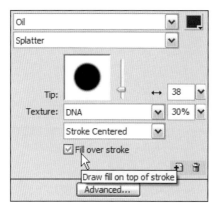

7 In the Layers panel, unlock and unhide the detective object, and position the shape you created below it in the stacking order. This puts the detective in front of the shape.

8 Save the file.

▶ **Tip:** Dragging layers up and down in the Layers panel moves them away or toward the front of the canvas, respectively. You can also choose Modify > Arrange, and then choose one of the four options to alter the stacking order of selected objects: Bring to Front, Bring Forward, Send Backward, and Send to Back. If you use this feature frequently, memorizing the keyboard shortcuts (Ctrl+Up/Down arrow for Windows, or Command+Up/Down arrow for Mac) will be a great time-saver.

Next you will import the movie title.

Importing and resizing a vector object

The movie title is a vector object. You'll import it and then scale it to fit the design.

1 In the Layers panel, select the custom path shape you created in the previous exercise.

2 Choose File > Import, and browse to the Lesson05 folder.

3 Select the movie_title.fw.png file, and click Open.

4 Make sure Insert after current page is *not* selected and then click Import (Windows) to return to the canvas. On the Mac, click Open, then click Open again (Mac). The import tool icon replaces the standard cursor.

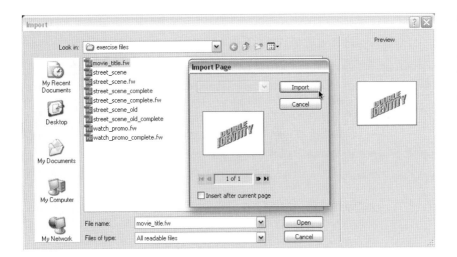

Note: When importing images in Fireworks on the Mac, you may have to click once on the canvas to make it active, then click a second time to import the image.

5 Click anywhere on the canvas to import the title at its original size.

6 In the Properties panel, lock the proportions of the object.

7 Set the width to **390** pixels.

8 Press the Tab key and the height adjusts automatically, giving you dimensions of 390 x 286 pixels.

9 Use the Pointer tool to position the title so the letter "Y" is near the brim of the detective's hat. The *x* and *y* coordinates should be around 178 x 183.

Note: Did you notice that the movie title's overall quality did not change after resizing? That's because the title is made up of a group of vectors. And, to ensure that the text style does not change from designer to designer, the text was converted from true text to paths.

Using the Compound Shape tool

You have one last task for this file. Notice the skyline scene? The client has asked that the entire width of the design be filled with a skyline, so you need to add one more building.

Rather than creating a single complex custom path, you will use the Compound Shape tool to temporarily group multiple vector shapes together as you draw them, making it easy to move the objects at the same time, yet also allowing for quick and easy editing of any shape within the compound group. You can also test effects such as punching, intersecting, or cropping overlapping vectors. When you use the Subselection tool ( ), each vector is easily accessible and editable.

Note: Yes, you could just copy one of the existing buildings, but you already know how to copy and paste!

Applying a pattern to a vector object

Adding a pattern works much the same way as adding a gradient. The available preset patterns are arranged alphabetically in the Fill Category Pattern submenu in the Property selection list (or you can create your own). They are bitmap images that have been designed to seamlessly tile inside a vector shape.

1 Create an exact copy of the custom shape by choosing Edit > Clone.

2 Choose Pattern > Wood from the Fill Category menu in the Properties panel.

As with the gradient, the control arms allow you to change the direction of the pattern or even distort it.

3 Place the cursor over one of the arms (not the points) to rotate the pattern to suit the orientation of your object.

4 Delete the object from the Layers panel.

▶ **Tip:** The Path panel (choose Window > Others > Path) opens up a lot of possibilities for creative design, even if you are not a whiz with the Pen tool. You can punch out corners, knock holes out of a shape, distort existing paths, and have a great degree of control over anchor points.

Working with compound shapes

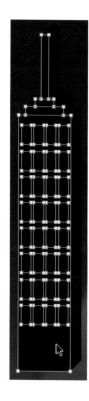

Before you begin, take some time to study one of these compound shapes.

1 Lock and hide the foreground layer, then unlock and expand the skyline layer.

2 Select the Pointer tool and click on the leftmost building. Notice that it is made up of multiple shapes.

3 Select the Subselection tool and click on any of the windows in the building. Notice that only the selected window remains active; none of the other shapes remain selected.

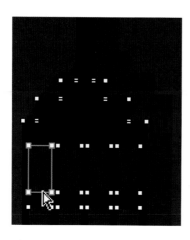

4 Press Delete. Only the one shape is removed.

5 Press Ctrl/Command+Z to undo the deletion.

6 With the window still selected, look to the right side of the Properties panel.

The Compound Shape tool consists of six controls: Normal, Add/Union, Subtract/Punch, Intersect, Crop, and Combine. Normal is the default setting; each drawn shape is a single independent object. When you draw a vector shape such as a rectangle, ellipse, or polygon, or use the Pen tool, you can use the other tools to group shapes together.

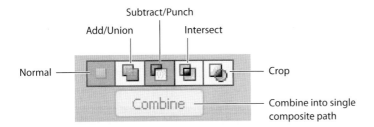

The rectangles that make up the windows are set to Subtract/Punch, which means they literally punch a hole through the larger rectangle of the building.

7 Change the condition of the selected rectangle from Subtract/Punch to Intersect. The entire building fill color disappears and only the single window (with its solid shadow effect) remains visible. In fact, if you click away from the building, you will see only the one rectangle, floating on the canvas.

8 Make sure the window is selected and change the shape's condition back to Subtract/Punch.

Adding to the skyline

Now it's time to add the new building.

1 Click away from the current building and make sure nothing else is selected.

2 Choose the Rectangle tool from the Vector tools section of the Tools panel, and near the right side of the canvas, draw a rectangle that is 106 pixels wide by 500 pixels tall.

3 Select the Zoom tool and draw a marquee that includes the top of the large rectangle and some space above it.

4 Select the Rectangle tool again. Then, in the Properties panel, click the Add/Union icon.

5 Draw a second, short rectangle at the top of the first one. Don't worry about position or size; you will adjust that next.

If you switch to the Pointer tool, you will see that both rectangles are selected.

6 Choose the Subselection tool and click on the small rectangle.

7 Drag the small rectangle until it sits flush on the top of the larger shape and is centered side to side. Smart Guides will help you with this positioning.

8 Repeat steps 5–7, this time drawing a slightly smaller rectangle. The Add/Union attribute remains in place until you deselect the current compound shape.

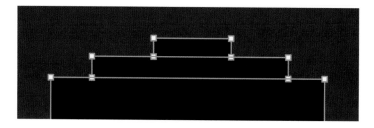

9 Zoom out until you can see the entire building.

Adding windows to the building

Note: Selecting the compound shape is just a way to make sure you are adding the other shapes to the correct object. Once you choose the Rectangle tool, the compound shape is no longer selected. This is normal.

It's time to add the windows. We'll make use of the History panel to speed up this process, but first we need to create one set of windows.

1 Make sure your building is still selected and then choose the Rectangle tool again if necessary.

2 Change the Compound Shape tool attribute to Subtract/Punch and draw a rectangle that is 20 x 40 pixels. When you release the mouse, a hole is punched through the main rectangle. Remember you can always adjust the dimensions in the Properties panel.

Note: The act of punching one vector through another can also be done using the Path panel or the Modify menu, but doing so requires multiple steps and is a destructive process. Punching one vector through another is normally a three-step operation: draw the punching shape, select both shapes, and then use the Path panel or Modify menu to perform the action. This workflow permanently changes the vectors by combining them into a single composite path. You did the same thing in just two steps, and the objects remain unique and editable!

3 Using the Subselection tool, position the rectangle about 13 pixels from the left edge and 26 pixels from the top edge of the main rectangle.

4 Press Ctrl+Shift+D (Windows) or Command+Shift+D (Mac) to create a clone of the window.

5 While holding down Shift, press the Down arrow key five times.

6 Open the History panel (choose Window > History) and locate the last two steps, Clone and Move.

7 Hold down the Shift key and click on Clone and Move to select them both.

8 Press the Replay button six times to create your first column of windows.

9 Choose the Subselection tool, and while holding down Shift, click on all of the windows to select them.

10 Clone the selected group of windows.

11 Hold down Shift and press the Right Arrow key three times.

12 Repeat steps 10 and 11 using the new column of windows.

13 Select the Pointer tool and drag your new building until the bottom lines up with the bottoms of the other buildings. Again, Smart Guides display a horizontal dashed line when the building matches up with the others.

14 One last step is to apply the solid shadow to this new building. Make sure the object is selected with the Pointer tool, and then choose Shadow And Glow > Solid Shadow from the Live Filters menu in the Properties panel.

15 Leave the Angle and Distance settings as they are, but enable the Solid Color option.

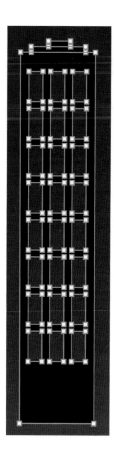

16 To make sure the new shadow has the same color as the others, click on the Color fill box and then place your cursor over one of the other shadows and click to sample that color exactly. Until you add the correct solid color, the whole object turns black.

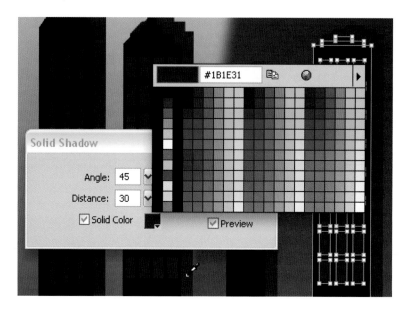

17 Click OK.

Your skyline is complete!

18 Unhide the foreground layer and save your file.

This has been a big lesson, but vectors are a large part of the creative toolset in Fireworks and it's important that you get comfortable with the tools. Although we did not work with the Auto Shapes panel, we recommend you have a look at the panel and check out the prebuilt vector shapes that are included with Fireworks.

Review questions

1 What is one of the main differences between bitmaps and vectors when scaling is applied?

2 When drawing a rectangle, how can you easily round the corners of the shape?

3 What are Auto Shapes, and where can you find them?

4 How do you edit the control points of a vector object once it has been drawn?

5 What is the Pen tool used for?

6 What does the Compound Shape tool do?

Review answers

1 Vector images do not degrade in quality when they are resized, either smaller or larger, and bitmap images do.

2 Before releasing the mouse, press the Up Arrow key to increase the roundness of the rectangle's corners. Press the Down Arrow key to reduce the corner radius.

3 Auto Shapes are objects that include additional diamond-shaped control points that let you alter visual properties, such as corner roundness. Dragging a control point alters the associated visual property. Most control points have tooltips that describe how they affect the Auto Shape, too. Basic Auto Shape drawing tools are found in the Tools panel; more complex ones are found in the Shapes panel.

4 To edit the control points of an existing vector object, select the Subselection tool, click on a control point, and drag the control point to reposition the paths connected to it.

5 The Pen tool lets you create custom shapes and paths by drawing with the mouse or a stylus. It also allows you to add anchor points to existing paths. Using the Pen tool involves clicking the mouse to set a straight line between two anchor points (a place where the path can change direction) or clicking and dragging to create a curved section of a path. Every time you want to change the direction of a path, you move the mouse to the desired position and then click to set another anchor point.

6 The Compound Shape tool lets you create complex vector shapes by temporarily grouping other, simpler shapes together, while maintaining the editability of each individual shape. You can quickly and easily experiment with various vector effects such as punching or intersecting, without having to walk through a series of destructive steps.

6 MASKING

Lesson overview

Masking is a key technique for creating imagery, without permanently affecting images. Combined with stroke effects and gradient fills, you can achieve customized results. Fireworks lets you work with both bitmap and vector masks easily and seamlessly. In this lesson, you'll learn how to do the following:

- Create a bitmap mask from a selection

- Edit a bitmap mask using the Brush tool

- Create a vector mask from a custom vector shape

- Edit the vector mask and change its properties using the Properties panel

- Use the Auto Vector Mask command

 This lesson takes approximately 90 minutes to complete. Copy the Lesson06 folder into the Lessons folder that you created on your hard drive for these projects (or create it now, if you haven't already done so). As you work on this lesson, you won't preserve the start files. If you need to restore the start files, copy them from the *Adobe Fireworks CS5 Classroom in a Book* CD.

Masking opens up a world of creative options and adds flexibility to your designs as well, because you are not permanently deleting pixels—you're merely hiding them from view.

About masks

In this lesson, you will work with masks to create a banner ad for the promotion of the Double Identity movie, and you'll have a chance to brush up on importing images and using the Pen and Subselection tools along the way.

Before we get into that, we'll talk about the differences between the two types of masks, and take a look at the finished artwork to give you an idea of where you're going.

1 Open the movie_banner_final.fw.png file from the Lesson06 folder.

   In this file, masks have been used on the cars and the actors. In many cases, the mask fill has been changed to a gradient, to provide a more realistic fade into the background.

2 Close this file, or keep it open for reference as you progress through the lesson.

In a nutshell, masks hide or show parts of an object or image. At their simplest, masks are a nondestructive way of cropping objects in your design, without permanently deleting anything. A mask can be edited or discarded at any time. You can also permanently apply a mask, flattening it to the image being masked. There are two basic kinds of mask: bitmap and vector.

Bitmap masks

Bitmap masks hide bitmap image data using a pixel-based mask. You can create bitmap masks using other bitmap images, selections, or the Brush (![brush icon]) tool.

To create a selection for a mask, you can use any of the bitmap selection tools. Decide on the type of edge you want for the selection (Hard, Anti-alias, or Feather) using the Live Marquee settings in the Properties panel. Then, just draw your selection. Bitmap selections can create masks only for other bitmaps.

▶ **Tip:** You can also mask one bitmap image with another. The darker tones in a photo used as a mask will hide areas on the image being masked. Lighter tones reveal parts of the masked image.

Using the Brush tool, you can easily create or edit the mask live on the canvas, just by painting. Black hides, white reveals, and shades of gray produce semitransparency. (We'll remind you of this important basic concept later in the lesson.) If you set your brush color to a shade of gray, the pixels you paint over will be semitransparent.

Creating a bitmap mask
with the Brush tool

Original image

Beginning to paint a
bitmap mask using the
Brush tool and black for
the brush color

The final masked image

Vector masks

Vector masking is one of the most powerful features in Fireworks. Like bitmap masks, vector masks are a nondestructive way of cropping, but unlike bitmap masks, vector masks can be applied to vectors, bitmaps, groups, or graphic symbols.

Compared to bitmap masks, vector masks tend to have a higher degree of control and accuracy, because you use a path, not a brush, to create them. It's easy to change the fill or stroke of a vector mask. Generating the same type of effect with a bitmap mask can be more time consuming.

Vector masks use one of two modes: Path Outline or Grayscale Appearance. You can change the mode in the Properties panel.

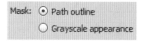

In Path Outline mode, the vector mask acts like a cookie cutter, using the shape of the path to act as the mask.

In Grayscale Appearance mode, any bitmap information in the vector fill gets converted to a grayscale alpha channel. Grayscale Appearance uses the pixel values of the vector's fill *and* the vector shape itself to create the mask. If your vector mask has a range of tones in it—such as a gradient fill—the image will be hidden or revealed based on those tones. Just like with bitmap masks, black hides, white reveals, and shades of gray produce semitransparency, as in this example, where a linear gradient has been used to fill the vector shape.

The convenient Auto Vector Mask command works in this way as well. We'll try that out later in the lesson.

You can easily apply a shape as a mask, whether you drew a vector shape using a shape tool or used the Pen tool to create a custom shape.

Designing the banner ad

The banner you build in this lesson has many elements to it—imported assets, masks, gradients, text, layers, and so on.

Creating the document

Start by creating the new, basic document to hold all your further work.

1 Choose File > New.

2 In the New Document dialog box, set the dimensions to **728** pixels wide by **90** pixels high. This is a standard horizontal *leaderboard* banner size.

3 Click the color swatch to set a custom canvas color.

4 Choose black (#000000) from the color picker and click OK.

Ultimately, this document will use multiple layers. You will add those now.

5 Double-click the existing Layer 1 name in the Layers panel and rename it **background**.

6 Click the New/Duplicate Layer icon ( ) at the bottom of the Layers panel.

7 Name the new layer **main**.

8 Repeat step 6 to create one more layer, and name it **text**.

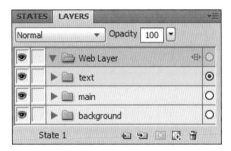

9 Save your file as **movie_banner_working.fw.png**.

Adding the background

The background for the final banner is not just a flat color; it's got some depth and variation in tone. You will create that now.

1 Lock the text and main layers by clicking the empty box beside the layer names. This will force any new objects into the background layer.

2 Select the Rectangle tool, and draw a rectangle the same size as the canvas (728 x 90 pixels).

3 In the Properties panel, set the X and Y coordinates to 0.

4 In the Properties panel, change the Fill Category to Gradient > Starburst.

5 Click the Fill color box to open the Gradient editor.

Editing gradient colors

Now you will set the colors for
the gradient.

1   Click the far-left color swatch.

2   Use the Eyedropper tool to select
    the black color swatch.

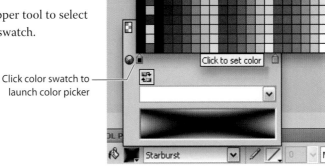

Click color swatch to
launch color picker

3   Add a new swatch by clicking just below the gradient ramp, where your
    cursor becomes an arrow with a plus sign next to it. A new gradient color
    swatch appears.

4   Click the color swatch, change the existing color value in the field to **#535973**,
    and press Enter or Return.

5   Continue adding color swatches to the gradient by typing the following values
    into the field: **181C25**, **000000**, **6A7295**, and **323647**.

6   Place the color swatches so that they resemble this figure, and click away from
    the Edit Gradient pop-up window when you've finished.

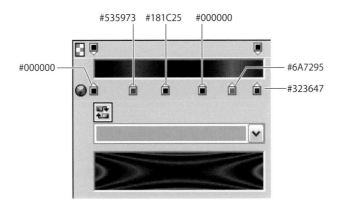

Editing gradient direction and angle

You can alter the angle and direction of a gradient by moving the gradient control arm (or arms).

With the rectangle still active, and the gradient applied, you should see two control arms. The arms are normally black, but we've outlined them in white here to make them easier to see.

Controls origin/position of gradient

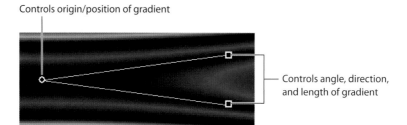

Controls angle, direction, and length of gradient

1 Select the Pointer tool from the Tools panel.

2 Change the length and angle of the upper gradient arm by dragging the square control point until it is similar to what you see here. Again, we have outlined the control arms in white so it's easier for you to see the change.

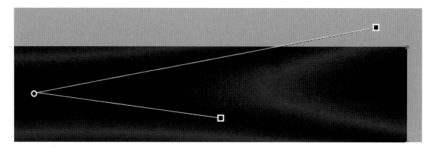

3 Rename the rectangle **background**.

4 Lock the background layer.

5 Save your file.

Importing assets

▶ **Tip:** When importing Fireworks files, remember you will have to click Open, then Import (Windows) or click Open, then Open again (Mac). Make sure that Insert After Current Page is not selected.

You're ready to import the movie title and cars now.

1 Unlock the text layer by clicking the lock icon beside the layer name.

2 Choose File > Import.

3 Open the movie_title.fw.png file in the Lesson06 folder.

4 When the import icon () appears, position the cursor near the left side of the canvas. Drag until the width is approximately 160 pixels and the height 78 pixels. Tooltips do not appear when you are scaling an imported image, so keep an eye on the Properties panel.

▶ **Tip:** On the Mac, you may have to click once to bring the canvas back into focus, then click a second time to import the image.

5 Release the mouse. The text appears.

◗ **Note:** This text is actually a series of paths that have been grouped together.

6 In the Properties panel, set the x and y coordinates for the title to **30** and **3** pixels, respectively.

7 In the Layers panel, rename the object **movie title**.

8 Lock the text layer, and unlock the main layer.

9 Choose File > Import, locate the policecar1.fw.png file, click Open, and then Import (Windows) or Open and then Open (Mac).

10 Drag the import icon until the width is approximately 80 pixels, and release the mouse.

▶ **Tip:** If you don't get the dimensions you want, you can constrain proportions in the Properties panel and enter the values numerically. Because the movie title is all vectors, enlarging it will not affect the quality of the grouped object.

11 In the Properties panel, set the x and y coordinates to **157** and **44** pixels, respectively.

12 In the Layers panel, rename the object **car1**.

13 Import the policecar2.fw.png file.

14 Release the mouse when the width reaches approximately 56 pixels. Set its x and y coordinates to **217** and **24** pixels, respectively.

15 In the Layers panel, rename the object **car2**.

Using the Auto Vector Mask for quick fades

You'll do more complicated masking shortly, but for these police cars, the Auto Vector Mask is just the feature to use. It not only creates a mask quickly, but lets you preview the effect. This command can be used on vector or bitmap objects.

1 Select car1 in the Layers panel.

2 Choose Commands > Creative > Auto Vector Mask. A dialog box appears.

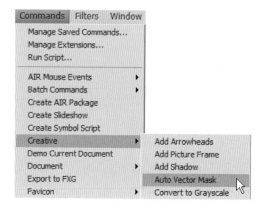

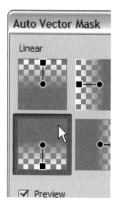

3 Choose the vertical linear gradient, solid to transparent.

4 Move the dialog box so it is not covering the car, so you can see the effect previewed on the canvas.

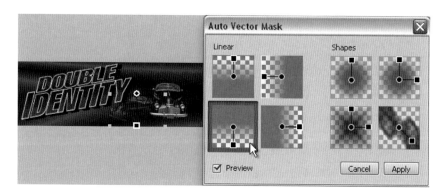

5 Click the Apply button.

6 Use the Pointer tool to reposition the gradient so it begins lower on the car. Place the circle control handle on the hood.

7 Drag the square control handle up and slightly to the right, to shorten the gradient and change the angle. The bottom front wheel of the car should appear to fade into the background.

▶ **Tip:** If you accidentally click off the car, clicking the gradient thumbnail in the Layers panel will retrieve the control handles again.

8 Select car2 from the Layers panel, or use the Pointer tool to select it on the canvas.

9 Choose Commands > Creative > Auto Vector Mask again.

10 Select the Radial shape gradient, and click Apply.

11 Use the Pointer tool to reposition the gradient circle control handle on the right side of the hood.

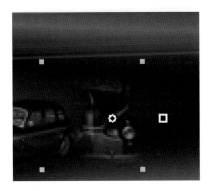

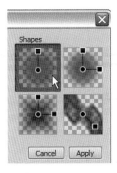

12 Drag the square control handle to the lower right. This will fade the top and left sides of the car, blending it with the other car and the background.

▶ **Tip:** Thanks to the Live Preview of the Auto Vector Mask effects, not only can you see the result of your choice before you apply it, the Properties panel also shows you what type of gradient is being used to create the effect.

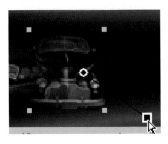

13 Save the file.

Importing Photoshop images

You are getting *lots* of practice importing images. You will import two more images now, but there's a twist. These images are Photoshop (PSD) files. Fireworks has some special features for importing such files, even if the file is only a single image.

1 Choose File > Import, and browse to the Lesson06 folder.

2 Open the mark_actor06.psd file. The Photoshop File Import Options dialog box appears. This dialog box contains many settings, but you are only concerned about image size at this time.

3 Set the width to **340** pixels. The height adjusts automatically. Click OK.

4 When the import icon appears, click on the canvas once to load the image at the dimensions you set.

5 Reposition the image to X: 97, Y: –45 pixels.

6 Rename the image in the Layers panel to **Mark**.

7 Lock and hide the Mark object.

8 Choose File > Import again.

9 Open the wendy.psd file.

10 Set the width to **290** pixels, and click OK.

11 When the import icon appears, click near the middle of the canvas once to load the image at the dimensions you set.

12 Rename the object in the Layers panel to **Wendy**.

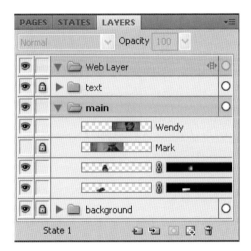

▶ **Tip:** Remember, importing files into an open document saves you the time of opening, copying, and pasting one image into another.

Opening Photoshop Files

Opening layered Photoshop files within Fireworks is as simple as choosing File > Open or File > Import and browsing for the native Photoshop PSD file. Fireworks CS5 supports hierarchical Photoshop layers, layer groups, layer styles, layer comps, vector layers, and common blend modes, making it easy to handle files you receive from another designer.

Exceptions to this integration include adjustment layers and clipping groups. These features can either be flattened into bitmaps or ignored when you import or open a PSD file within Fireworks. Flattening retains the appearance, but editability is lost.

continues on next page

Opening Photoshop Files *continued*

To globally customize how Fireworks opens or imports PSD files, change the preferences. Choose Edit > Preferences (Windows) or Fireworks > Preferences (Mac), and then select Photoshop Import/Open from the list on the left.

The General Photoshop Import options include:

- Show import dialog box/show open dialog box. These identical windows give you document-level import/open control.

- Share layer between frames. This option is important for animation or "page state" effects.

The custom file conversion settings area includes the following options:

Image layers:

- Bitmap images with editable effects. This option is the default setting that gives you the most flexibility. Layer styles remain editable.

- Flattened bitmap images. This option flattens layer effects and blend modes to maintain the exact appearance. Photoshop layer styles are no longer editable.

Text layers:

- Editable text. This option is the default.

- Flattened bitmap images. This option preserves the look and style of text, but the text is no longer editable.

Shape layers as:

- Editable paths and effects. This is the default option with the most flexibility, but vectors may not render exactly as in Photoshop.

- Flattened bitmap images. When this option is enabled, vectors and effects are rasterized to bitmaps.

- Flattened bitmap images with editable effects. When this option is enabled, vectors are rasterized but layer effects and blend modes remain editable.

Layer effects:

- Prefer native filters over Photoshop live effects. This option is only recommended if the file will not be going back to Photoshop.

Clipping path masks:

- Flatten to maintain appearance. When this option is enabled, the mask is converted to a bitmap mask.

Adjustment Layers:

- Maintain appearance of adjusted layers. This option flattens adjustment layers to retain the image's appearance, but you can no longer edit the image. If this option is not selected, adjustment layers are discarded completely.

With the defaults left as they are, opening or importing a PSD file displays the Photoshop File Open Options or File Import Options dialog box. This gives you the opportunity to set options for opening a specific PSD file, overriding any options set in the Preferences panel.

Note: A Photoshop layer comp is essentially an editable snapshot of the current state of the design. It's similar to pages in Fireworks in that each layer comp can show a different set of visible elements or different positions for those elements.

Creating and editing masks

You've now come quite a long way with the banner ad file, and a lot of the assets are in place—enough for you to notice that there is far too much background visible in both of the actor photos. You will use masks to hide most of those backgrounds.

Creating a vector mask

Comparing the completed version with your working version, you can see that Wendy is facing the opposite direction from Mark. You will alter your image of Wendy so she faces the same direction as the finished file.

1   Select the Wendy image.

2   Right-click (Windows) or Control-click (Mac) Wendy's face on the canvas. A context menu appears.

3   Choose Transform > Flip Horizontal.

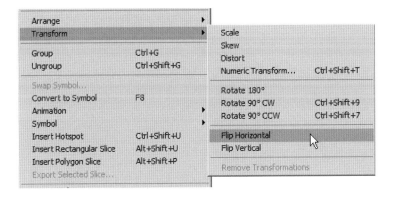

4   Set the position to X: 340, Y: −39.

5   Select the Ellipse tool from the Tools panel.

6   Change the edge from Anti-alias to Feather, with a value of 10, if necessary.

7 Draw an oval shape around Wendy's face, approximately 90 x 106 pixels. The ellipse should be roughly centered on her face.

8 Release the mouse. The vector ellipse appears, filled with the last Fill Category option used for a vector. The category needs to be a gradient ellipse; if this is not what shows up in the Fill Category field, choose Gradient > Ellipse from the Fill Category menu.

9 Select the Fill color box and change the gradient in the Fill Color box to the White, Black preset.

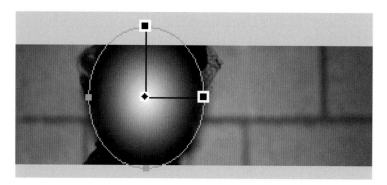

10 Select the Pointer tool.

11 Hold down the Shift key and select the Wendy photo. Now both objects should be selected.

12 Choose Modify > Mask > Group As Mask.

The ellipse now masks the photo of Wendy. The small blue handle in the center of the masked image allows you to reposition the image within the mask, by dragging with the Pointer tool.

Changing vector mask attributes

As you learned earlier, Grayscale Appearance mode uses the pixel data of the vector fill to alter opacity. That's why the image of Wendy fades out around the edges. Combined with the feathered edge, you get a subtle blend into the background. You will edit the angle and length of the gradient now.

1   Select the mask thumbnail next to the Wendy image in the Layers panel.

The Ellipse shape appears on the canvas and the Gradient fill control arms appear.

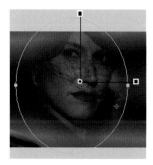

2 Use the Pointer tool to move the circle control point of the gradient so that it is near her nose. You will find this easier to do if you zoom in to at least 200%.

3 Use the Pointer tool to set the arms to a clock position of roughly 4:35.

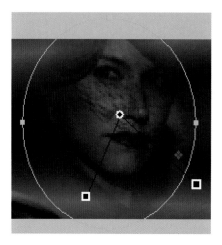

▶ **Tip:** Once a mask has been added, you can reposition the image being masked by dragging the small blue control icon (🔷) in the middle of the image. This icon is visible when the image object, rather than the mask, is active.

4 Extend the left arm slightly out of the canvas area.

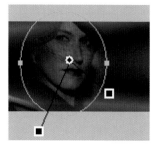

5 Hide and lock the Wendy object.

Editing a vector mask

When a vector mask is made active from the Layers panel, you can use the Properties panel to change the Fill Category and Edge settings, as well as those of the stroke (category, size, and edge).

You edit the vector shape itself by choosing the Subselection tool and repositioning the vector control points, just as you would with a regular vector shape. You can even add points by using the Pen tool. For more information on editing vectors, refer to Lesson 5.

Converting a bitmap selection to a mask

Sometimes cropping and masking go hand in hand. If you have a small area that you want to mask within a larger image, it may be a good idea to first crop out the unnecessary parts of the larger image. For the Mark image, you won't need the surrounding background at all, so you will crop the image first, and then make a selection mask.

1 Unlock and reveal the Mark object in the Layers panel.

2 Choose Edit > Crop Selected Bitmap.

3 Adjust the cropping marquee so that you exclude the background on either side of the detective, and then press Enter or Return.

4 Reposition the image to approximately X: 215, Y: −45. The exact position will vary depending on how much you cropped the image.

5 Select the Polygon Lasso tool ( ).

6 Make sure the Lasso edge is set to Feather, with a value of **5**. The Live Marquee can remain selected.

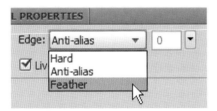

Note: To refresh your memory on how to use the Lasso tools, you may want to review Lesson 4 before proceeding.

7   Zoom in on the detective's face and trace a selection around him. Don't be concerned if the selection is not 100 percent accurate; you will remedy this in the next exercise.

8   Click the Add Mask button () at the bottom of the Layers panel. The background disappears from the Mark object.

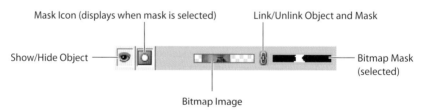

Editing a bitmap mask

Notice that the mask object has a green highlight around it in the Layers panel. Additionally, the mask icon appears beside the object name. This indicates that the mask—and not the image—is active.

Mask Icon (displays when mask is selected)   Link/Unlink Object and Mask

Show/Hide Object ——————   —— Bitmap Mask (selected)

Bitmap Image

It is important that the mask remain active while you are performing these next steps. If at any time the mask is deselected, just click on it in the Layers panel.

Take a look at the mask. The color black has replaced the nonselected area. Remember that the color black, when painted on a bitmap mask object, hides pixels. White, on the other hand, reveals pixels. You will adjust the mask as needed using the Brush tool.

1   Zoom in to 200%.

2   Select the Brush tool.

3 Press the D key to set the brush color to black (the default color).

4 Make sure the Stroke Category is set to Soft Rounded (if necessary, choose Basic > Soft Rounded from the Stroke Category pop-up menu).

5 Change the Tip Size value to **10** pixels and the Edge to **100** pixels. The Texture value should be 0%.

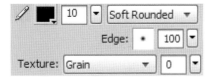

6 Paint over any areas of the background that remained when you drew the original bitmap selection with the Polygon Lasso tool.

7 Press the X key to switch the brush color to white.

8 Find an area on the actor that was masked by accident. Paint over the area. The mistakenly hidden pixels are revealed.

If you end up revealing areas you don't want, switch back to black and paint over those areas.

● **Note:** If you didn't make any mistakes while creating the selection, you can still test this technique by painting over part of the background. The area under the brush reappears when you paint with white, and disappears when you paint with black.

Changing colors quickly

When working with bitmap masks, you may want to switch from black to white to gray to customize the mask. You can do this quickly with these shortcuts:

- Press the B key to switch to the Brush tool.
- Press the D key to set the color boxes to their default colors (black for stroke, white for fill).
- Press the X key to toggle the current colors between stroke and fill.

Applying Live Filters to a masked image

To give the two actors a darker, grittier, and mysterious look, you will apply a Live Filter to each of them. Remember that the advantage to Live Filters is that they remain editable at all times.

1   Reveal and unlock the layer named Wendy.

2   In the Layers panel, drag the Wendy layer underneath the Mark layer. Mark is large in the design, so it makes more visual sense to have him in the foreground, in case of any overlap between the two actor images.

3   Hold down the Shift key, and use the Pointer tool to select both actors.

4   Click the Add Live Filters (+) button in the Filters category of the Properties panel, and choose Adjust Color > Brightness/Contrast.

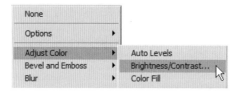

5   Set the Brightness to -**20** and the Contrast to **20**, and then click OK. Because both images were selected, the effect is applied simultaneously to both.

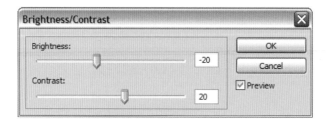

If the settings are not to your liking, select one of the objects, and then click the *i* icon beside the Live Filter name in the Properties panel. The dialog box will open again, and you can edit the settings.

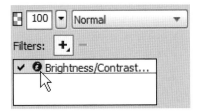

Adding the silhouette

Your last graphical touch will be adding in the silhouette of a man.

1 Choose File > Import.

2 Open cameo.fw.png.

3 When the Import icon appears, click on the canvas to load the image at its original size.

4 In the Properties panel, set the *x* and *y* coordinates to **611** and **-1** pixels, respectively.

5 Save the file.

Final touches

There are several finishing touches you have to add to this design: you'll put in some more text, tweak the position of some objects, and add an accent highlight behind the movie title.

Adding text

First you will add the promotional text.

1 Lock the main layer, and unlock the text layer.

2 Select the Text tool.

3   Select the following settings in the Properties panel:

Font Family: Arial

Font Style: Bold

Font Size: 12 points

Color: White

Anti-aliasing: Strong Anti-alias

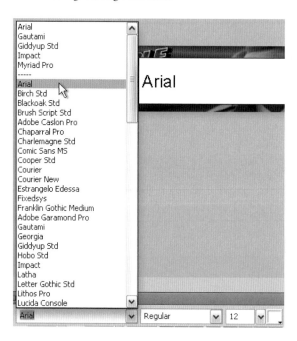

4   Move the cursor to the canvas just below the movie title.

5   Type **COMING SUMMER 2010**.

6   Double-click "2010" to select the year.

7   Choose Brush Script or a similar sketch-like font from the Font Family menu.

8   Triple-click anywhere on the text to select the entire text block.

9   Hold down Shift + Ctrl (PC) or Shift + Command (Mac) and tap the right arrow key once, to increase the tracking between each character by 100.

10 Use the Pointer tool to reposition the text box so the first word is below the E of "Identity" in the movie title.

Adding the cast names

The main stars of the movie are important, too, so you will add those now.

1 Make sure the font is set to Brush Script (or a similar sketch-like font) and that the Font Style is set to Bold. If Bold isn't available, click the Faux Bold icon (B). Change the size to 20 points. The size may vary depending on your font choice.

2 Move the cursor between the Wendy image and the silhouette.

3 Type **Mark**.

4 Set the position to X: 519, Y: 3 in the Properties panel.

5 Move the cursor away from the text box, and click on the canvas.

6 Type **Wendy**.

7 Set the position to X: 519, Y: 43.

8 Select the Text tool again and click on the canvas to start a new text block.

9 Choose Arial Black with font size 28. Then, type **SOUSA**.

10 Set the position to X: 507, Y: 17 in the Properties panel.

11 Click on the canvas again, and type **CARTER**.

12 Set the position to X: 502, Y: 59.

13 Adjust the first names so they appear slightly above the last names.

Styling the text

Now you'll spice up the text of this banner ad a little bit by changing its fill.

1 Zoom in to 300%.

2 Select the Pointer tool, and then select SOUSA.

3 Open the Text Color box, and click the Fill Options button.

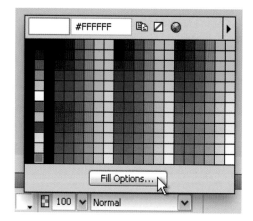

4 Choose Gradient from the Fill Category menu, Linear from the gradient type menu, and White, Black from the gradient preset menu; then press Enter or Return.

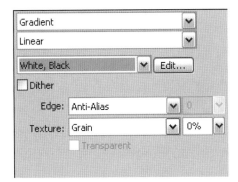

5 Reposition and shorten the gradient control arm so that it extends over the text only, rather than the entire text box.

Creating a custom style

You're going to use this gradient effect again, so it's a good time to create a custom style.

1 Make sure the text block is still selected, and open the Styles panel by double-clicking on the panel tab or by choosing Window > Styles.

2 Click the New Style icon (▣) at the bottom of the Styles panel. The New Style dialog box appears.

3 Deselect all the text properties.

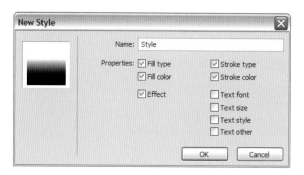

4 Name the style **Movie Text**, and click OK. The new style appears in the Current Document section of the Styles panel.

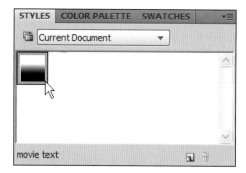

Note: Custom styles remain available to any object in the document from which they were created. To make a custom style available to other documents, you must export it. To learn about exporting styles, see Adobe Fireworks Help.

5 Select the Pointer tool.

6 Select CARTER.

7 Click on the newly created style. The selected text block receives the same treatment as the SOUSA text.

Styling the first names

You will keep things simple for the first names.

1 In the Layers panel, rearrange the layers so that the names Mark and Wendy are stacked above the two last names.

2 Hold down the Ctrl (Windows) or Command (Mac) key, and select the Mark and Wendy objects in the Layers panel.

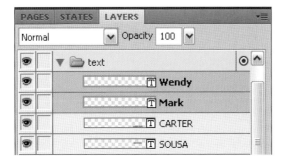

3 Change the text color to #**CCCDDA** in the Properties panel.

4 Select the Scale tool from the Tools panel.

5 Position the cursor just outside of the scaling handles to the right of the text.

6 When the cursor changes to a rotate icon, click and drag upward just slightly.

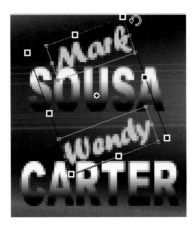

7 Press Enter or Return to commit to the rotation.

8 In preparation for the next exercise, hide and lock the text and main layers, and unlock the background layer.

9 Save the file.

Tweaking the background

The background fill has a nice look, but it's a bit dark. You will adjust this now.

1 Select the background rectangle.

2 Click the Add Live Filters (+) button in the Filters category of the Properties panel, and choose Adjust Color > Brightness/Contrast. The Brightness/Contrast dialog box appears.

3 Set Brightness to **20** and Contrast to **0**, and press Enter or Return.

4 Select the Ellipse tool from the Vector section of the Tools panel.

5 Draw an oval that is 135 pixels wide by 84 pixels high. Don't worry about the fill color for now.

6 Set the position to X: 14, Y: 3.

7 Hold down the Alt (Windows) or Option (Mac) key, and press the right arrow key. This creates a duplicate of the oval.

8 Select the Pointer tool and drag the new oval to the right so that it slightly overlaps the first ellipse. Smart Guides help you align them at their top edges. Final positions should be X: 14, Y: 3 and X: 126, Y: 3.

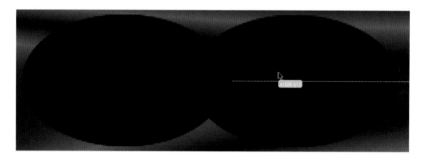

9 With both ovals highlighted, choose Add/Union from the Compound path tool in the Properties panel.

10 Click the Combine button in the Properties panel. This joins the two separate ellipses into a single path.

11 In the Properties panel, set the edge to Feather, with a value of **22** pixels.

Note: If you have multiple color swatches in the gradient, choose the Black, White preset before setting the custom colors listed in steps 13 and 14.

12 Change the Fill Category to Gradient > Ellipse.

13 Click the Fill Color box to open the Edit Gradient pop-up window. Click the left color swatch, and choose black from the color picker.

14 Click the right color swatch, and then click the eyedropper on a bright area of the background rectangle in the file to set the new color.

15 Press Enter or Return.

16 Reposition the gradient to the right, as shown here.

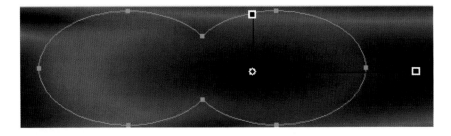

Image positioning

Before you wrap up, you will do a final check on the image locations and save the file.

1 Unlock the main layer.

2 Select the Mark image.

3 Confirm that its position is approximately X: 211 and vertically centered. The actual X coordinate may vary depending on how you cropped the photo.

4 Select the Wendy image.

5 Reposition the image to approximately X: 340. Her face should be a little above vertical center and just to the right of the detective's face.

6 Save the file—you're done!

Review questions

1   What are the primary differences between bitmap masks and vector masks?

2   How do you use the Auto Vector Mask?

3   How do you create a vector mask?

4   How do you create a bitmap mask?

5   How do you create a custom style?

Review answers

1   Bitmap masks are made using selections or the Brush tool. Using the Brush tool, you can easily edit the mask live on the canvas. Bitmap masks can be applied only to other bitmaps. Vector masks tend to have a higher degree of control and accuracy because you use a path, not a brush, to create them. It's easy to change the fill or stroke of a vector mask. Generating the same type of effect with a bitmap mask can be more time consuming. Vector masks can be applied to bitmap or vector objects.

2   The Auto Vector Mask can be applied to bitmap or vector objects. Select the object on the canvas, and then choose Commands > Creative > Auto Vector Mask. Choose the type of mask from the dialog box, and then click Apply.

3   To create a vector mask, draw a vector shape, then hold down Shift and select the object to be masked. Choose Modify > Mask > Group as Mask. You can select the mask in the Layers panel, and change its fill, edge, and stroke properties. You can also use the Pen tool or Subselection tool to edit its shape.

4   You create a bitmap mask in one of two ways:

   • Draw a bitmap selection, select the object you want to mask from the Layers panel, and click the Add Mask button in the Layers panel.

   • Select the object you want to mask from the Layers panel, and click the Add Mask button in the Layers panel. Select the Brush tool, setting the brush color to black, and then paint on the canvas. As long as the mask object is selected, painting with black will hide pixels from view.

5   To create a custom style, select an object that has Live Filters or fill and stroke attributes applied to it. Click the New Style icon in the Styles panel. Select the properties you want to maintain, deselect those you don't, and name the style.

7 WORKING WITH TEXT

Lesson overview

Fireworks CS5 uses the same text engine as Photoshop and Illustrator, which makes moving or copying between these applications fairly straightforward. Aside from the improved text handling between applications, working with type can be a fun and creative part of your design.

Fireworks includes many text-formatting features normally found in desktop publishing applications, such as kerning, spacing, color, leading, and baseline shift. You can edit text any time—even after you apply Live Filter effects. In this lesson, you'll learn how to do the following:

- Create both fixed-width and auto-sizing text blocks
- Edit text properties
- Use commands to alter text
- Scale, rotate, and distort text
- Use text as a mask
- Attach text to a path
- Flow text within a vector shape

 This lesson takes approximately 60 minutes to complete. Copy the Lesson07 folder into the Lessons folder that you created on your hard drive for these projects (or create it now, if you haven't already done so). As you work on this lesson, you won't preserve the start files. If you need to restore the start files, copy them from the *Adobe Fireworks CS5 Classroom in a Book* CD.

You don't need to settle for dull text. Fireworks includes the text-formatting features that help you get the look you want. You can make your text pop off the page with Live Filters, masks, and strokes, or even make a block of text flow within a custom vector shape.

Getting started

You will be working with a partially complete file for this lesson. The artwork is already in place; you just need to add some text elements.

1 In Fireworks, choose File > Open.

2 Browse to the Lesson07 folder, and open the movie_promo.fw.png file.

3 Choose File > Save As.

4 Save the file as movie_promo_fw_working.png.

Text basics

Text in Fireworks always appears inside a text block (a rectangle with handles). Text blocks can be either auto-sizing or fixed width.

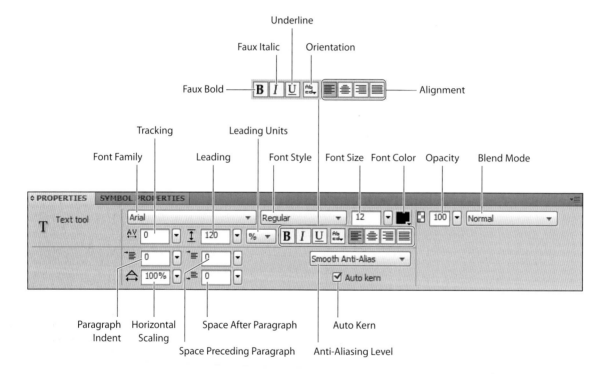

Creating an auto-resizing text block

When you click on the canvas with the Text tool and just start typing, Fireworks creates an auto-sizing text block, which expands horizontally as you type. Auto-resizing text blocks only expand vertically when you press the Return or Enter key.

1 Unlock the Text layer in the Layers panel.

2 Select the Text tool (**T**).

   When the Text tool is active, the Properties panel displays text attributes, such as font family, font style, size (measured in pixels), color, alignment, tracking, leading, indent, horizontal scaling, text indent, and paragraph spacing.

   You can also add a stroke color, stroke style, and Live Filters to text. You can change these settings before or after you have added text.

3 In the Properties panel, set the font family to Arial or another sans serif font like Helvetica.

4 Set the font style to Regular, the font size to 12 pixels, the color to Black, and Anti-Aliasing Level to Smooth.

5 Click anywhere on the canvas.

   Auto-sizing text blocks are created by default when you click on the canvas with the Text tool and start typing.

6 Type **He was called crazy, and he was . . . crazy like a fox**!

   Note how the text box expands horizontally as you type. It shrinks when you remove text, or adds lines automatically as necessary.

7 Place the text cursor before the letter *c* in the second instance of the word *crazy* and press Enter or Return.

> **Note:** Fireworks remembers the most recent fonts used by the Text tool, even after you've shut down and restarted your computer. They appear at the top of the font family list. You can change the number of recent fonts displayed by editing the Type preferences.

Creating a fixed-width text block

Fixed-width text blocks allow you to control the width of wrapped text. As you add more text, the box expands vertically. Fixed-width text blocks are created when you drag to draw a text block using the Text tool.

1 Move the cursor away from the first text block.

2 Drag a box that is about as wide as the previous text box. The exact size is not important. This is a fixed-width text block.

3 Release the mouse.

4 In the Properties panel, change the font family to Poplar Std or a similarly strong font.

5 Set the font style to Bold, the font size to 20 pixels, and the color to #64667F. Leave all the other settings as they are.

6 Type **A Film directed by Robert Legato**. Notice that the text wraps to the next line when you reach the right edge of the text box.

When the Text tool is active within a text block, a hollow square or hollow circle appears in the upper-right corner of the text block. The circle indicates an auto-sizing text block; the square indicates a fixed-width text block.

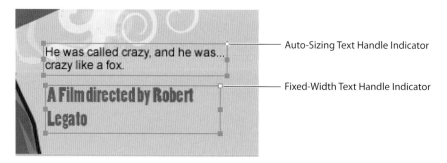

7 Make sure the text cursor is flashing in the text block. If it isn't, use the Text tool to click once anywhere in the text.

8 Double-click the hollow control point to change the new text box from a fixed-width block to an auto-sizing block. The text reflows into one line.

Editing text

You must select a text block or specific text within a text block to edit it or change its properties.

1   Select the Pointer tool, and make sure the most recent text block is active. Anything you change within the Properties panel or through text commands affects the entire text block.

2   Choose Commands > Text > Case Uppercase.

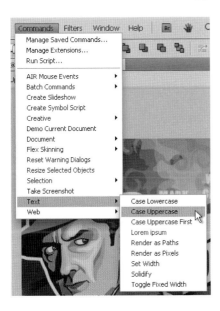

You can change parts of the text in a text block by selecting the text first.

3   Double-click inside the DIRECTED BY text block. This puts you in text-editing mode.

4   Select the words DIRECTED BY.

5   Change the font size to 12 pixels in the Properties panel.

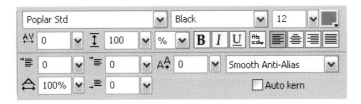

6 Switch back to the Pointer tool, and reposition the text to X: 379, Y: 369.

7 Select the first text block.

8 Change the font family to Poplar Std or a similarly bold font.

9 Change the font size to 28, the leading to 100, and make sure the text color is still set to Black.

Note: When you edit a text block, each change during that edit session is considered a separate step, making it easy to undo individual changes.

10 For now, change the position of the text block to X: 303, Y: 264.

11 Save the file.

Flowing text within a vector shape

In sophisticated page layout software such as Adobe InDesign®, you can wrap text around an object. You can achieve this effect in Fireworks CS5 by inserting text within a vector shape.

1 In the text layer, hide the first text object you created, which contains the words *He was called crazy...* by clicking the eye icon.

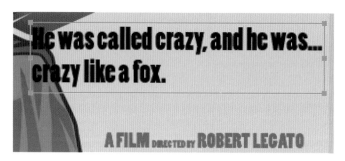

2 Select the Pen tool (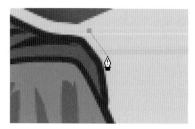).

3 Click once to set a control handle near the shoulder of the detective.

4 Continue clicking with the Pen tool as you follow the contour around the detective's shoulder, and then move across to the right and click to create a straight bottom, straight up the right side, and then back across to the left for the top. Remember, each time you want to change direction, click the mouse to set a control point.

5 Click on the starting control handle to close the path. The final shape should be similar to what you see here.

6 Make both the fill and the stroke of the path transparent by setting their colors to None in the Properties panel.

7 Reveal the text ("He was called crazy") you hid in step 1.

8 Select both the shape and the "He was called crazy" text block in the Layers panel.

9 Choose Text > Attach In Path. The text reflows within the vector shape.

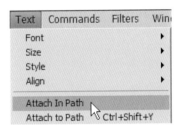

● **Note:** If you are having trouble creating this shape, we've created it for you; just unlock and reveal the object called "crazy path."

10 Change the Paragraph Indent value to 10. This pushes the paragraph 10 pixels to the right from its original starting point.

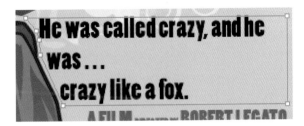

Text attached in a path—or to it—remains editable at all times.

Note: If you create a shape with one of the Auto Shape tools or the Rectangle tool, you first have to ungroup the shape before you can attach the text within it. Choose Modify > Ungroup to do this.

Note: If you have more text than can fit inside a vector shape (or on a vector path), Fireworks hides the extra text and displays the Text Overflow indicator. In order to see the extra text, you must either increase the size of the vector or reduce the size of the text.

11 Place the text cursor after the comma and press Enter or Return.

12 Select the word *fox* and then in the Properties panel, add faux italic styling by clicking the I icon (*I*).

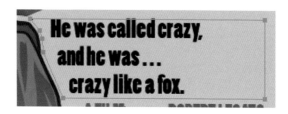

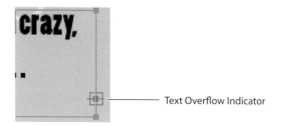

Text Overflow Indicator

Typography terms

Let's look at some typography terms you should be familiar with:

Kerning: Adjusts the space between letters based on character pairs. There is strong kerning (more space) between the letters V and A, for example, and no kerning between the letters S and T. You can turn Auto Kerning on or off in the Properties panel.

Tracking: Unlike kerning, tracking adds equal amounts of space between all selected characters.

Leading: Also known as line spacing, leading is the amount of vertical spacing between lines of type. The word comes from the lead strips that were put between lines of type on a printing press to fill available space on the page.

Horizontal Scaling: Adjusts the width of each selected character or characters within a selected text box.

Baseline Shift: Controls how closely text sits above or below its natural baseline. For example, superscript text sits above the baseline. If there is no baseline shift, the text sits on the baseline. To adjust baseline shift, select the actual text (not the text box) and input a value into the Baseline Shift field in the Properties panel.

Paragraph Indent: Sets the amount of indent for the first line in the paragraph.

Paragraph Spacing: Sets the amount of spacing before and after a paragraph in a selected text block. Any value set here is respected by all paragraphs within a text block.

Note: As of this writing, you may experience text issues when opening a file created in versions of Fireworks earlier than CS4. Text must be updated when opening a legacy file to minimize issues.

Anti-aliasing

Text anti-aliasing controls how the edges of the text blend into the background so that large text is cleaner, more readable, and more pleasing to the eye. Fireworks examines the color values at the edges of text objects and the background they are on. It blends the pixels at the edges based on the anti-alias settings in the Properties panel.

By default, Fireworks applies smooth anti-aliasing to text. However, small font sizes tend to be easier to read when anti-aliasing is removed. Anti-aliasing settings apply to all characters in a given text block.

Anti-alias settings

Fireworks provides four preset anti-aliasing levels and a custom setting:

- **No Anti-Alias:** Disables text smoothing completely. Text is not blended, and anything but horizontal or vertical lines are noticeably jagged. Although not ideal for large text, it can actually make text at small sizes (8 point or less) easier to read.

- **Crisp Anti-Alias:** Displays a hard transition between the edges of the text and the background. Some blending occurs, but text still appears sharp.

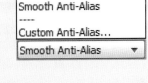

- **Strong Anti-Alias:** Creates an abrupt transition between the text edges and the background, preserving the shapes of the text characters and enhancing detailed areas of the characters. Text appears almost bold in comparison to Crisp Anti-Alias.

- **Smooth Anti-Alias:** Creates a soft blend between the edges of the text and the background, and is the default for text pasted into Fireworks.

- **Custom Anti-Alias:** Applies the settings you select from the following options:

  Oversampling: Sets the amount of detail used for creating the transition between the text edges and the background.

  Sharpness: Sets the smoothness of the transition between the text edges and the background.

  Strength: Sets how much the text edges blend into the background.

Changing anti-aliasing

The text you formatted seems a bit fuzzy against the solid color background. The other preset anti-alias settings do not improve matters significantly, so you are going to apply custom anti-aliasing to this text.

1 Select the Pointer tool, and click the crazy text block to make it active.

2 Change the Anti-Alias setting to Custom Anti-Alias, using these values:

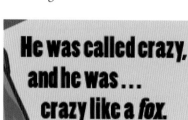

- Oversampling: **16 times**
- Sharpness: **100**
- Strength: **0**

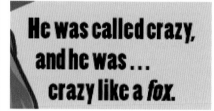

Smooth Anti-aliasing   Custom Anti-aliasing

3 Select the Pointer tool and click off the canvas to ensure nothing is selected.

Special text effects

There are several kinds of effects and changes you can apply to text to jazz it up.

Attaching text to a path

Attaching text *to* a path—as opposed to *in* a path—lets you put text on an angle, or even follow a curve.

1 Select the Text tool.

2 Set the font size to 24 pixels in the Properties panel and if necessary, deselect the italics and bold icons.

3 Click on the canvas, and type **COMING SUMMER 2010**.

4 Select the Pointer tool and drag the text block to X: 327, Y: 237.

5 In the Properties panel, change the horizontal scaling to 109% and the color to #DAEEFA.

Now you can create the path.

6   With the Pen tool ( ), click at the bottom edge of the red banner to set a starting point.

7   Follow the angle of the red banner, and click one more time to set a stopping point for the path.

If you move the cursor again, notice the Pen tool is still active, dragging a new path segment. You need to disengage the Pen tool and stop the path.

8   Select the Pointer tool and the Path snaps back to a single, selected segment.

9   Hold down the Shift key, and select the COMING SUMMER 2010 text block. Holding Shift lets you select multiple objects on the canvas.

10 Choose Text > Attach To Path. The text follows the angle of the path (and remains editable).

▶ **Tip:** If you have more text than can fit on the path, that extra text will disappear, and a text overflow indicator will appear at the end of the path. Select the Subselection tool, and drag the end control handle of the path to make it wider. Your text reappears.

The vertical skew of the text doesn't match the movie title. You will alter this now.

11 With the text object still selected, choose Text > Orientation > Skew Vertical.

12 Reposition the text object, if necessary, and save the file.

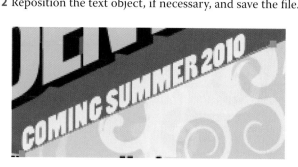

Skewing text on an angle

Another way to change the angle of text is to use the Skew tool. In this file, where the cast names are all in separate text blocks, it is easier to change the angle in this manner rather than attaching each text block to its own vector path.

1 Press the Shift key, and select each actor name.

2 Open the Align Panel (Window > Align).

3 Click the Align Bottom Edge icon (▨).

4 Choose Evenly from the Space area, and click the Space Evenly Horizontally icon (▥).

5 Select the Skew tool (hidden beneath the Scale tool) from the Tools panel.

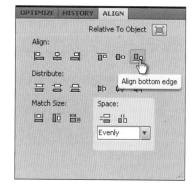

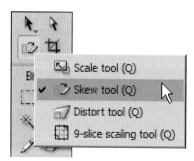

6 Move the cursor over the middle control handle on the right side of the selected block of text.

7 Click the mouse and drag upward until you match the angle of the movie title text.

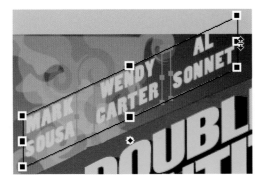

8 Release the mouse to apply the skew.

Using text as a mask

You will add two more special effects to cast names to add some more pizzazz. First, you'll create a text mask effect. This effect uses the text outline to mask another object.

1 Select the Rectangle tool (▣) from the Vector section of the Tools panel.

2 Draw a rectangle large enough to cover all three cast-member names.

3 For the Fill, choose Gradient > Linear.

4 Select the Fill Color box and select the Silver preset gradient.

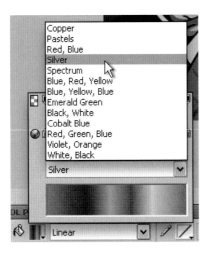

5 Move the rectangle below the cast names in the Layers panel.

6 Deselect the rectangle.

7 Press the Shift key, and select all three cast names.

8 Choose Edit > Cut.

9 Select the rectangle.

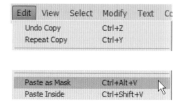

10 Choose Edit > Paste As Mask.

The gradient rectangle is now masked by the text.

11 Click on the text, using the Pointer tool. The gradient control arm appears.

▶ **Tip:** The text remains editable as a mask. Just select the Text tool and click on the text to go into text-editing mode.

12 Drag the square control handle for the gradient to the right so that the gradient runs at approximately the same angle as the text. Drag the square upward to shorten the length of the gradient. You want some contrast between the text and the background.

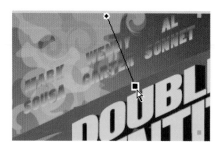

Adding Live Filters to a masked object

Notice the hard, solid shadow on the movie title? To quickly add a similar effect to the masked gradient, use the Solid Shadow Live Filter. Once applied, Live Filters remain editable so you can adjust the filter or even remove it without damaging the original object.

1 If necessary, select the masked rectangle.

2 Click the Add Live Filter (+) button in the Filters category of the Properties panel and select Shadow And Glow > Solid Shadow.

3 Set the Angle option to **335**.

4 Set the Distance value to **8**.

5 Select the Solid Color checkbox and change the Fill color to #3B3F5A. We determined this number by moving the cursor over the dark blue background and clicking the mouse.

6 Click OK and save the file. You're done!

▶ **Tip:** You can tell which object (mask or maskee) is active by looking at the Layers panel. The highlighted object is the one that is active.

Review questions

1 What are the two types of text blocks you can create, and how do you create them?

2 What is anti-aliasing?

3 How do you flow text within a path?

4 How can you quickly select a single paragraph in a text block?

5 What typographic attributes can you control using the Properties panel, and how do these elements affect text?

Review answers

1 You can create auto-sizing and fixed-width text blocks. Auto-sizing text blocks are created by default when you select the Text tool, click the canvas, and begin typing. Auto-sizing text blocks expand in width as you add more text. Fixed-width text blocks are created by dragging out with the Text tool on the canvas before typing. Fixed-width text blocks allow you to control the width of wrapped text. As you add more text, the box expands downward.

2 Text anti-aliasing controls how the edges of the text blend into the background so that large text is cleaner, more readable, and more pleasing to the eye.

3 Draw a vector shape using the vector shape tools or the Pen tool. Select both the vector shape and the text, and then choose Text > Attach In Path. If you create a shape with one of the Auto Shape tools or the Rectangle tool, you will first have to ungroup the shape before you can attach the text within it. Select the Auto Shape and then choose Modify > Ungroup to do this. Once text is attached in a path, it still remains editable.

4   You can quickly select a single paragraph in a text block by triple-clicking anywhere inside the paragraph.

5   Kerning, Tracking, Leading, Horizontal Scaling, Baseline Shift, Paragraph Indent, and Paragraph Spacing can all be controlled from the Properties panel.

- Kerning adjusts the space between letters based on character pairs. You can turn Auto Kerning on or off in the Properties panel.

- Tracking adds equal amounts of space between all selected characters.

- Leading, also known as line spacing, is the amount of vertical spacing between lines of type.

- Horizontal Scaling adjusts the width of each selected character or characters within a selected text box.

- Baseline Shift controls how closely text sits above or below its natural baseline. To adjust Baseline Shift, select the actual text (not the text box) and input a value into the Baseline Shift field in the Properties panel.

- Paragraph Indent sets the amount of indent for the first line in the paragraph.

- Paragraph Spacing (two settings) sets the amount of spacing before a paragraph (preceding) and after a paragraph in a selected text block.

8 OPTIMIZING FOR THE WEB

Lesson overview

Fireworks has its roots in web graphics. And with web graphics, you have to balance quality and file size. Optimization reduces the amount of time a web browser takes to download and display those images.

In previous lessons, you learned the basics of working with graphics in Fireworks. Now you'll apply those skills to creating and optimizing assets for web pages, and for web-page creation itself. In this lesson, you'll learn how to do the following:

- Export a single image to a web-ready format

- Determine the optimal web format for a sliced graphic

- Use the Optimize panel and Preview views to optimize images

- Slice up graphics in a web-page mockup using the Slice tool

- Create a rollover effect using the Slice tool

- Add a hyperlink using the Hotspot tool

- Export an interactive mockup of a website

- Export a single page as a standards-based CSS and HTML web page

 This lesson takes approximately 90 minutes to complete. Copy the Lesson08 folder into the Lessons folder that you created on your hard drive for these projects (or create it now, if you haven't already done so). As you work on this lesson, you won't preserve the start files. If you need to restore the start files, copy them from the *Adobe Fireworks CS5 Classroom in a Book* CD.

Fireworks does many things, but at its roots it is a web graphics application—be it for creating mockups, editing screen-resolution images, exporting graphics to the Flash platform, or optimizing and exporting images to CSS and HTML.

5 Zoom in to 150% and look closely at the gradient between Wendy's face and the actor names. The effect isn't as smooth as in the Original view. The effects appear banded.

GIF files can display up to 256 color values and, as a result, don't do a good job of rendering many gradient effects.

6 Look at the bottom-left corner of the document window. The status bar displays export file information. Here it reads "30.62K 4 sec @56kbps GIF (Document)." (These file sizes may differ slightly on your system.) This file information area, also visible in Original view, tells you the file size and the download time of the image if it is exported as a GIF file.

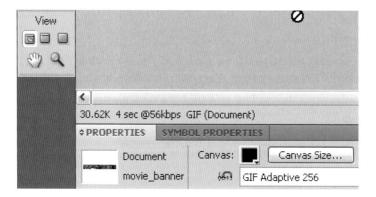

7 In the Optimize panel, choose JPEG – Better Quality from the Saved Settings pop-up menu. Recall that JPEG is usually a much better option for exporting an image with gradients and a wide color range.

The gradient smoothes out in the banner ad. Equally—if not more—important is the updated information in the status bar of the document window: 18.09K 2 sec @56kbps. The image quality has improved, and the file size has decreased.

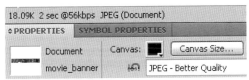

8   Zoom out to 100% and select the 2-Up view. The document window splits into two panes. On the left, the Original view is displayed. On the right, the current optimization settings for the image are displayed. The 2-Up view is helpful when comparing differences in quality between the original design and an optimized version.

9   Select the Pointer tool and click on the right pane. A border appears around that window, indicating it is the active window.

10 In the Optimize panel, change the Quality setting to 60. You can change the value by typing it in and pressing the Tab key (or Enter or Return) or by dragging the slider. (When you type the value, there is a slight delay before the preview updates with the new quality setting.) The file size decreases to approximately 11.34K.

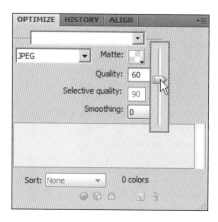

Note: If you use the N-Up feature (the ability to dock multiple windows to the application frame), each document window offers its own Original, Preview, 2-Up, and 4-Up views.

11 Zoom in to 150%, if necessary, and compare the two versions of the movie title (Original and Preview). The panes are synchronized, so as you zoom or pan in one window, the other displays exactly the same view.

If you study the movie title closely in the Preview version, you will see that the background surrounding the text is not as smooth as it is in the Original view. What you see here is the result of the JPEG quality setting. These JPEG artifacts become more visible as you reduce the image quality of the file.

Choosing optimization settings

Comparing the potential exported image to the original is important, but there are subtle changes in the Optimize panel that can make a big difference to the final exported file. You'll now experiment with the other preview options.

1 Zoom back out to 100%. Even at this 1:1 magnification, the artifacts are still somewhat visible and may be unacceptable to you or a client.

2 Click the 4-Up button. The document window is now split into four previews, with the Original view remaining in the top-left corner.

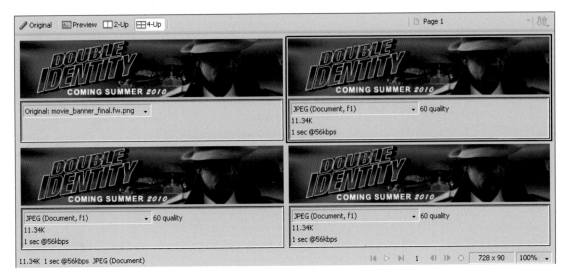

3 Select the bottom-left preview, and change the Quality setting to 80 in the Optimize panel.

4 Select the bottom-right preview, and change the Quality setting to 70.

You can now compare three different quality/compression previews to the Original view. By comparing these versions of the same file, you can quickly determine the best combination of file size and image quality.

5 Zoom in to 150%, and compare the three JPEG versions against the original image. Bearing in mind that none of them will be quite as good as the original, try to determine which of the three is most suitable. The 80% quality looks good, but it's just over 18K. The 60% quality is a great file size, but the artifacts are pretty noticeable. So it looks like 70% could be the winner. But you're not done yet.

6 Change the 60% and 80% previews to 65% and 75%, and inspect them again.

The 75% Quality setting seems to give the best combination of file size and image quality.

7 With the 75% Quality preview selected, click the Original button. The document window displays a single view, and the settings you selected remain in the Optimize panel.

Note: Understand that, to a degree, optimization is a subjective choice, especially when you're dealing with small changes in quality or file size. If you're designing a site for an intranet, you have a little more leeway with your decisions about file size and quality.

▶ **Tip:** The JPEG format can compress areas of solid color too much, and because text is often a solid color, the quality of text can suffer noticeably. If you have large text—or a great deal of text—in your design, you can sometimes improve the text quality by enabling the Selective Quality setting in the Optimize panel, and selecting the Preserve Text Quality option. We didn't use this option to improve quality in the banner because of the resulting increase in file size.

Exporting the file

The final step is to export the Fireworks PNG file as a JPEG file. While a Fireworks PNG file can be displayed by web browsers, it contains information not necessary to a web-page image, such as layers, objects, and effects, which can make the file size quite large. JPEG files, on the other hand, are flattened images, which you can further reduce in file size by adjusting the quality settings of the file.

1 Choose File > Export.

2 Browse to the Lesson08 folder.

3 Change the filename to **movie_banner.jpg**.

4 Choose Images Only from the Export menu, if it is not already chosen.

5 Leave the Include Areas Without Slices and Current Page Only options selected.

6 Click Save (Windows) or Export (Mac).

7 When you return to the canvas, save the file so that the settings you made in the Optimize panel remain with it, and then close the file.

About the web tools

To produce compositions in Fireworks that make their way into a web page, you need to be familiar with the available web tools.

You'll find a number of web-related tools in the Tools panel:

- The three hotspot tools let you draw rectangular, circular, or polygonal shapes over portions of your image. When exported with HTML, hotspots link to other web pages or trigger other events on a web page, such as a remote rollover.

- The Slice tool ( ) and the Polygon Slice tool ( ) let you cut a larger image into smaller pieces, or select which parts of a web-page prototype will be exported as graphics for a web page.

- The Hide Hotspots and Slices button ( ) hides slices and hotspots.
- The Show Hotspots and Slices button ( ) makes slices and hotspots visible.

Creating and optimizing slices

A slice is a portion of an image or design that you intend to export as a unique graphic. When exported as HTML and Images, individual slices can include interactivity such as image rollovers, hyperlinks, and remote rollovers. Slices are always added to the Web layer of a Fireworks document.

Each web slice has its own optimization settings. Without slices, your image or design has only one optimization setting applied to it, as in the first exercise in this lesson.

In this section you'll learn several ways to create slices, how to optimize the slices for various types of graphics, and how to name the slices.

Which slice tool do you choose?

You can choose from two slice tool styles: rectangle or polygon. Because web pages are essentially laid out in a grid format, you will most often use the standard (rectangular) Slice tool.

The Polygon Slice tool can be useful if you want a nonrectangular area to be interactive, but this tool uses HTML tables and hotspots as well as slices (the resulting exported file consists of rectangular slices in a table and a polygon hotspot).

You can't have true polygon-shaped images, just like you can't have elliptical-shaped images on a web page. Like it or not, everything ends up as a rectangle, because HTML uses *only* width and height for an image in a web page. If you use a lot of polygon slices, your HTML code can become quite complex and require more CPU processing time, thus slowing down the browsing experience.

Creating slices manually with the Slice tool

You will use the standard Slice tool to cut up a web-page mockup. Accurate slicing is important. If you are going to create manual slices, be sure to zoom to at least 150% or 200% to ensure your slice includes the entire area you want to export.

1   Open the check_mag_home_start.fw.png file from the Lesson08 folder. This is a completed web-page mockup.

2   Select the Zoom tool, and zoom in to the upper-left area of the design by dragging the zoom tool around the watch image. Zooming in helps you slice only the graphic and not any surrounding area.

3   With the Pointer tool, select the watch image. Make a note of its dimensions in the Properties panel (237 x 90 pixels).

4   Select the Slice tool, draw a box over the entire watch graphic, and then release the mouse.

A green translucent rectangle appears on top of the watch image.

A slice has three main components: the slice name (user-definable), slice selection handles (for resizing a slice), and the behavior handle for adding interactivity to a slice. Red slice guides also appear, showing you how Fireworks will automatically slice up the rest of the document.

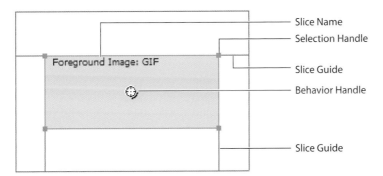

When it creates a slice, Fireworks automatically assigns the slice a name, based on the image's filename and future location inside an HTML table-based layout. These names become the actual filenames for the slices when they are exported. They can be fairly cryptic, and likely won't have any relevance to you later in the web production process. We recommend that you give meaningful names to all the slices you create.

5   In the Properties panel, double-click the slice name to select the entire name. Change the current slice name (check_mag_home_start_r2_c2) to **img_watch_ promo**. Note there are no spaces in this name. It's a good idea to use standard web-naming conventions with slices; avoid spaces and special characters, and— ideally—decide on and stick to a system for using upper- and lowercase letters. We keep things nice and simple by putting all web filenames in lowercase.

Now even without seeing a thumbnail of the file, you would easily know what this graphic is and where it's supposed to go on the web page.

Adjusting slice dimensions

If this is your first time creating a slice by hand, don't be surprised if you need to tweak the dimensions of the slice. When you zoom in, it should be easy to see if the slice is smaller or larger than the image behind it. If you need to make adjustments, you can either use the Pointer tool to resize the slice or change the dimensions numerically in the Properties panel.

Note: With the exception of button symbols, a slice object is not attached to the image below it, so if you reposition the image, you also need to reposition the slice.

Seeing web objects in the Layers panel

Slices and hotspots fall into the category of web objects. When you create either type of web object, Fireworks automatically places them in the Web layer of the Layers panel. The Web layer is always at the top of the Layers panel.

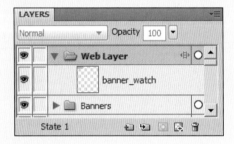

Optimizing a sliced image

This image is also a photo, which means—for optimization purposes—the format should be JPEG.

1 In the Optimize panel, make sure the slice is set to JPEG – Better Quality. Then, click the 2-Up preview button at the top of the document window.

Notice that everything except the watch seems to be grayed out in the preview window. When you preview a design with multiple slices, only the selected slice (or slices) appear normal, so you know which part of your design you are optimizing. Likewise, the optimization information in the preview window is specific to the watch slice.

2   Change the Quality setting to **40**. Note that the only area that changes in quality is the watch.

3   Change the Quality setting to **70**.

4   Click the Original button.

Adding more slices

The beauty of slices is that you can have different formats, and even different optimization settings, in a single design. This gives you the flexibility to truly optimize an entire page design in a single document, rather than having multiple separate image files. You will now add a new slice using an alternative method.

1   Select the Pointer tool.

2   Scroll down near the lower-right corner of the design, and select the illustration of the race-car driver.

3   Right-click (Windows) or Control-click (Mac) the image, and choose Insert Rectangular Slice from the context menu. (Hotspots can also be created in this manner.)

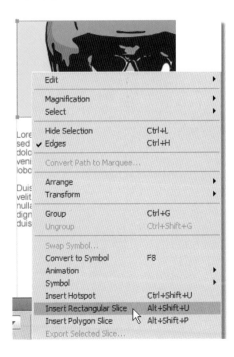

A slice is automatically added, based on the object's dimensions.

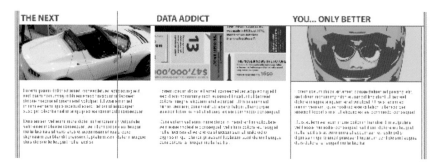

4   In the Properties panel, change the slice name to **img_racer.**

Optimizing illustrations

Images that are made up of solid colors need different optimization settings than JPEG to get the best results. For our racer image—the slice you just created—your best format option is either GIF or PNG 8, both of which handle solid colors quite well and will compress this image better than the JPEG format. In this exercise, you will discover which of these two formats does the best job.

1   Zoom to 100% so you can see the racer image at its normal size.

2   Select the 4-Up preview.

3   Holding down the spacebar, click and drag within any preview pane to pan over to the racer.

4   Click on the racer image within any of the preview panes to make sure it's active.

5   Select the upper-right preview pane, and choose GIF Adaptive 256 from the Saved Settings menu.

6   Set the Transparency option to No Transparency.

7 Select the lower-right preview pane, and set the format to PNG 8 from the Export File Format menu.

8 Make sure Indexed Palette is set to Adaptive and Colors to 256.

9 Set the Transparency option to No Transparency.

10 Note the file size for each. The PNG file should be about 1 KB smaller than the GIF.

PNG 8 is the way to go for this image.

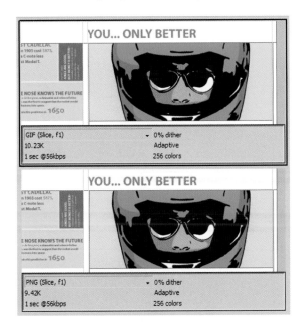

Reducing illustration file size

The main way to reduce file size in GIF or PNG 8 images is to reduce the number of colors used in the image.

1 Set all three previews to PNG 8.

2 Select the upper-right pane, and change the number of colors to 64 in the Optimize panel. Note the drop in file size.

Even at 64 colors (instead of 256), the image looks good, and the file size is pretty reasonable, too.

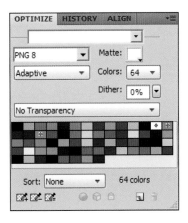

3 Make sure the Indexed Palette and Transparency settings are the same as the lower-right preview pane.

4 Now select the lower-right pane, and change the number of colors to **32** in the Optimize panel.

5 Make sure the Indexed Palette and Transparency settings are the same as the upper-right preview pane.

6 Change the number of colors in the lower-left pane to 16.

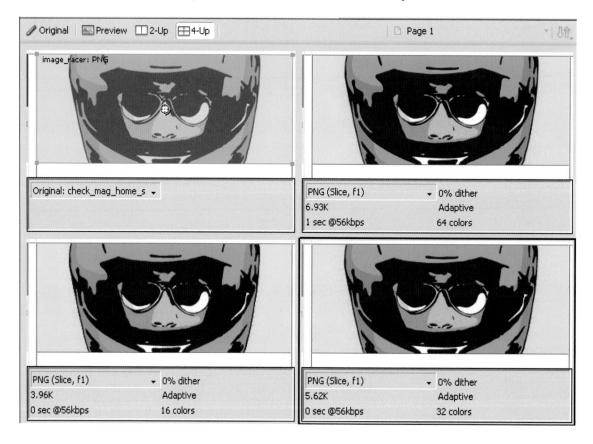

At this setting, the number of colors has been reduced so much the image is losing some of its subtle colors and tones, like the gray in the sunglasses.

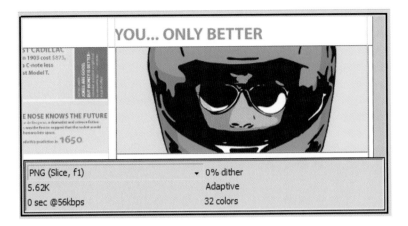

7 Select the 32-color window. To maintain color integrity, you may need to accept a slightly larger file size. You'll need to make decisions about balancing quality and file size for every asset you export.

8 Click the Original view button.

9 Save the file.

Slicing tricks for working with multiple items

You will add and format the final slices for this design. First you'll use a handy shortcut to create the rest of the slices.

1 Select the Pointer tool.

2 Hold down the Shift key, and click on the remaining five graphics in this layout.

3 Right-click (or Control-click) on any one of the selected objects.

4 Choose Insert Rectangular Slice from the context menu. This time a confirmation box appears, asking if you want to create a single slice or multiple slices from the selected objects.

5 Click Multiple. All five image objects get sliced. They will all have the same optimization settings that you just used in the previous example, and each will be auto-named by Fireworks.

6 Click outside the canvas to deselect all the slices.

7 Hold down the Shift key again, and select just the slices that overlay photos. These are the movie banner, the large photo of the actor, and the photo of the car.

This time, instead of using the Optimize panel, you'll set basic optimization options in the Properties panel.

8   Change the file format to JPEG – Better Quality in the Slice Export Settings menu in the Properties panel (below the Type menu).

9   Click outside the canvas to deselect all the slices.

Optimizing the illustrations

For the racer illustration, you were able to get a nice combination of image quality and file size using PNG 8. You'll change two more slices to that format. The PNG 8 setting is not available in the presets in the Properties panel, so you'll make the changes in the Optimize panel.

1   Hold down the Shift key, and select the navigation area slice and the illustration below the words DATA ADDICT. To make it easier, we've hidden all the slices you *don't* need to worry about in this illustration.

Tip: If you create a custom optimization setting, you can save it for use at a later time. Just choose Save Settings from the Optimize panel menu.

Note: Best practices today are to turn text links into true HTML text and control the color using CSS. You will learn more about this in the last exercise in this lesson.

2 In the Optimize panel, set the format to PNG 8.

3 Make sure Indexed Palette is set to Adaptive.

4 Hold down the Shift key and click on the DATA ADDICT slice. This leaves only the navigation slice selected. (Pressing Shift when you click on a selected slice deselects only that slice.)

5 In the Optimize panel, change the number of colors to **16**.

6 Set the Transparency option to No Transparency.

7 Set Dither to 0%.

8 If you see a button titled Rebuild, click it. This will remap the actual colors based on the value in the Colors field.

9 Select the slice below the heading DATA ADDICT.

10 Switch to the Preview view.

11 Set the number of colors to **32**.

12 Save the file.

Naming slices

It's easy to forget to rename slices, but it's a really good idea. You will name all those new slices now, before going any further. Remember, you can change the name of any slice directly in the Properties panel.

1 Select the slice that covers the movie banner image.

2 In the Properties panel, change the name to **img_banner.**

3 Select the slice covering the logo and navigation bar, and change the name to **img_nav.**

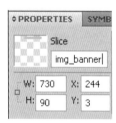

4 Select the slice covering the actor's photo, and rename it **img_main**.

You'll rename the last two slices in a different manner.

5 Open the Web layer in the Layers panel if it is collapsed. Collapse the Optimize panel by clicking on the gray bar next to the tabs if you need to free up more room for the Layers panel to expand.

6 Select the slice covering the car.

7 In the Web layer, locate the selected slice.

8 Double-click slice name, and change it to **img_car.**

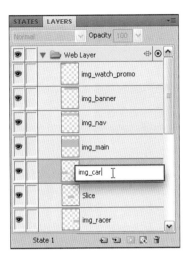

9 Select the slice covering the data illustration, and rename it **img_data.**

10 Save the file.

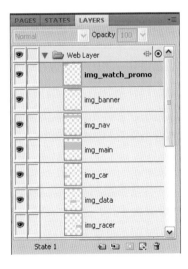

Creating a hotspot

▶ **Tip:** Although you should avoid overlapping slice objects, it is quite all right to place hotspot objects on top of slice objects. When you add hotspots on top of a slice, you're creating an image map.

You can use the various hotspot tools to create hyperlinks within any slice object. You'll add one hotspot to this design, on top of the img_nav slice.

1   Select the Rectangle Hotspot tool ().

2   Draw a box around the words FASHION + LIFESTYLE.

The Properties panel updates to display attributes for the hotspot.

3   In the Link field, type **http://www.adobepress.com/** and type **Visit the Website** in the Alt field.

Previewing the page in a browser (or uploading as a graphical web page) enables the link. When someone clicks the hotspot, they'll jump to the URL you've entered.

4   Save the file.

Previewing in a browser

Previewing in a browser gives you the opportunity to test interactivity (rollover effects, hyperlinks) and also lets you see how your choices for image optimization look within a browser.

● **Note:** The page is a true HTML page, but all assets, including text, are rendered as graphics. These previews are helpful when building site mockups or testing interactivity, but they should not be considered as the final web page.

1   Choose File > Preview In Browser, and choose your browser from the submenu. Depending on your computer setup, the browsers listed may vary. In our case, the default (Primary) browser was Firefox.

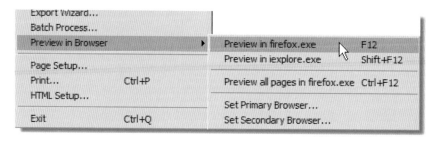

Fireworks loads the selected browser and loads a temporary copy of the web-page design.

2 Click on the FASHION + LIFESTYLE text. If you have a live Internet connection, the browser will load the home page for Adobe Press.

3 Close the browser.

4 Save the file in Fireworks.

If your design has multiple pages (we'll come to that in Lesson 10), you can create links from one page to another using hotspots or slices.

More on the Hotspot tool

Fireworks provides three hotspot tools: the Rectangle Hotspot tool ( ), the Circle Hotspot tool ( ), and the Polygon Hotspot tool ( ). You can quickly access the hotspot tools by pressing the J key. Like all multiple tool icons in the Tools panel, if you keep tapping the shortcut key (or hold down the left mouse button on the tool itself), you will toggle through all the available tools.

The Rectangle and Circle Hotspot tools are pretty self-explanatory, and produce fairly simple image map HTML code when a file is exported as HTML and Images. The Polygon Hotspot tool creates precise hotspot shapes around irregularly shaped objects. But the amount of HTML markup this type of hotspot produces is significant, so it's best to use the Polygon Hotspot tool sparingly.

Adding interactivity

Note: A Swap Image behavior is a prebuilt JavaScript used by Fireworks (and Dreamweaver) to create a rollover image effect. Behaviors do not require the user to know any JavaScript and can be customized using the Behaviors panel.

As with hotspots, you can add hyperlinks to slices. If you export a web-page design from Fireworks as HTML and Images, the URLs remain with the images. If you export an interactive PDF, again, those links will remain with the slices.

Slices can become rollover images, but hotspots cannot. Because a slice becomes a separate image, you can use built-in JavaScript behaviors within Fireworks to set up a Swap Image behavior. JavaScript rollovers were common in navigation bars not so long ago, but the use of CSS and background images has gained in popularity.

Note: A rollover image is a combination of images used to provide interactivity between the user and the web page. The term originates from the act of "rolling the mouse cursor over the image" causing the image to react (usually by replacing the image's source image with another image), and sometimes resulting in a change in the web-page itself.

However, JavaScript rollovers are quick and easy to do when creating a graphical website click-through. This way, you can easily show a client all the visual interactivity using JavaScript for the mockup, and then deal with coding the CSS rollovers later for the production site.

Here's how to create a simple rollover effect:

1 Open the check_mag_home_start.fw.png file if it's not already open.

2 Click the Hide Slices And Hotspots button in the Tools panel.

3 Hold down the spacebar, and then drag to pan down to the racer illustration.

4 Select the illustration of the racer.

5 Choose Edit > Copy.

6 Open the States panel.

7 Click the New/Duplicate State button to add a new, empty state.

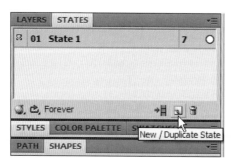

8 Choose Edit > Paste. The racer image appears in the same location as the original, but on (or in) this new state.

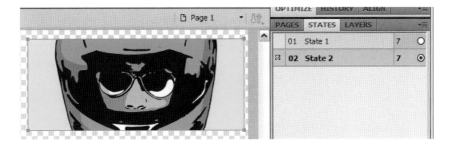

9 Select the racer image on the canvas.

10 Click the Add Live Filter button (+) in the Filters section of the Properties panel, and choose Adjust Color > Invert.

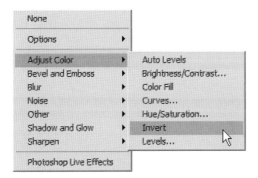

11 Click on State 1 in the States panel. The entire design reappears.

12 Reveal the slices by clicking the Show Slices And Hotspots button in the Tools panel.

13 Click the Behaviors handle on the img_racer slice, and choose Add Simple Rollover Behavior.

14 Click the Preview button at the top of the document window.

15 Move your mouse over the racer image, and watch it change.

16 Save the file.

Exporting composite designs

Fireworks has two main workflows for converting your visual concepts into web pages: you can export as HTML and Images or as CSS and Images.

Exporting HTML and images

The HTML And Images export option produces table-based HTML layout, which does an excellent job of matching your Fireworks design. It can also include hyperlinks and rollover effects. That's the good news.

Now for the bad news. This table-based layout is rigid; removing or adding elements to the page using a web-page editor like Dreamweaver can cause the table structure—and web-page layout—to break. By default, everything in the design is exported as an image, including the text.

From a best-practices perspective, you should avoid table-based layouts for your final websites, and learn how to use CSS for laying out final web pages.

That said, there is a place for this feature in the modern workflow. Many designers use the standard HTML capabilities in Fireworks for creating interactive graphical HTML prototypes for client feedback. It's a great way to test ideas and concepts without having to code any HTML right away. The client can request changes on the visual aspects of the design, and you can accommodate them without having to write a single line of HTML code—just update the design in Fireworks and export the file again. After prototype approval, you should code the final pages in a web editor such as Dreamweaver.

You will test out this export process now:

1 Open check_mag_home_start.fw.png if it is not still open.

2 Choose File > Export, and browse to the Lesson08 folder.

3 Create and open a new folder in the Lesson08 folder and call it **webpage**.

4 Change the Export field to HTML And Images.

5 Set the HTML field to Export HTML File, and the Slices field to Export Slices. Make sure the following three options are selected: Include Areas Without Slices, Current Page, and Put Images In Subfolder.

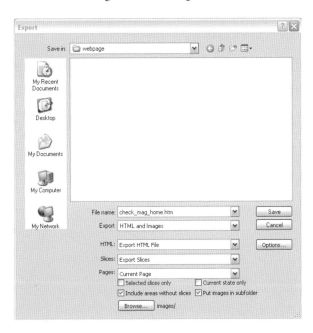

6 Click the Options button, and then the Table tab.

7 Make sure Space With is set to Nested Tables, No Spacers. This setting will maintain the layout without adding multiple transparent spacer images to hold everything together. All other settings can remain at the defaults.

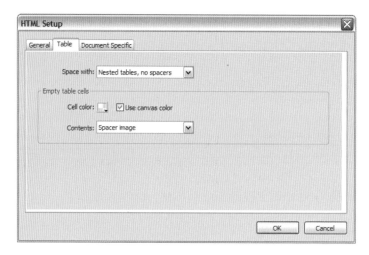

8 Click OK to close the Options dialog box, and then click Save (Windows) or Export (Mac) to create your web page.

9 Browse to the webpage folder using Windows Explorer or the Finder.

Inside the folder you will see the web page, check_mag_home.htm (or check_mag_home.html if you've previously altered the default file extension settings) and an images folder. These figures show the folder contents as displayed in the Finder (left) and Windows Explorer (right).

10 Double-click on the web-page to view it in your default browser.

11 Compare the web-page to the Fireworks PNG design; they appear very similar, if not identical. You can even click on the hotspot you created earlier over the words FASHION + LIFESTYLE and go to Adobe Press again.

12 Scroll down to the bottom of the web page, and try to select the text. You can't—because it's a graphic. The three blue headings are also one graphic.

13 In your browser, view the source code of the page. (In Firefox, choose View > Page Source.)

Fireworks added JavaScript to the head of the document, and the inline code in the body of the document that is necessary for the image swap.

14 Close the browser.

15 Open the images folder within the webpage folder.

Twenty-six images—many of which are solid-white images—were exported. For the Fireworks-generated HTML to display properly, all these images are needed.

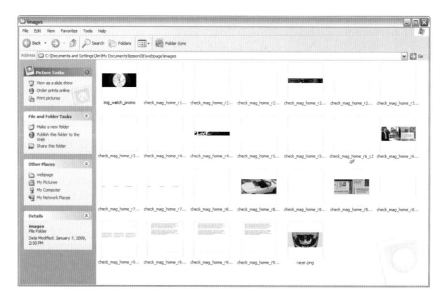

In actuality, there are only eight truly necessary images, if you were to build this page in a web editor such as Dreamweaver, or export as CSS and Images from Fireworks:

- img_watch_promo.jpg

- img_racer.png

- img_racer_s2.png (rollover image)

- img_car.jpg

- img_data.png

- img_main.jpg

- img_nav.png

- img_banner.jpg

Ideally, any text that was exported as images should be re-created as true text within Dreamweaver, and styled using CSS.

From a mockup perspective, this export is fine: it shows the client how the page will look and it's interactive. However, from a practical, end-user perspective, you would want to build the final web-page in a web-page editor.

16 Go back to Fireworks, and save the file.

Exporting states

Creating rollovers as you did earlier does present one problem at this time. If you choose to export the HTML and images, including all states, you end up with a bunch of unnecessary extra graphics. You see, Fireworks doesn't just export that one extra rollover image—it exports slices for *every* part of the design in that second state, even if there are no graphics!

The workaround for this is not elegant, but it works, and saves you from having to delete many unneeded graphics later on.

1 Reopen the images folder that you exported to previously, and delete all the graphics.

2 Return to Fireworks, and choose File > Export. Make sure the export file type is still set to HTML And Images.

3 Choose Export Slices from the Slices menu.

4 Make sure that the Include Areas Without Slices, Current Page, Put Images In Subfolder, and Current State Only options are all selected.

5 Click Save (Windows) or Export (Mac). Let Fireworks overwrite any existing files, if you are prompted to do so.

6 When the main document window appears, switch to State 2 in the Layers panel and then select the image_racer slice.

7 Right-click (or Control-click) on the slice, and choose Export Selected Slice.

8 Browse to the image folder within the webpage folder.

9 Change the Export option to Images Only, if necessary.

Note: There have been some enhancements to the HTML setup. You can now customize the filenames for states. You can set this up by choosing File > HTML Setup and clicking the Document Specific button. A file must be open in Fireworks in order to access this menu item. You can also click the Options button when you are exporting a file, and click the Document Specific button.

Note: When you export all states of a multistate file, Fireworks—by default—appends the file names with _s1, _s2, and so on, including the main state. This ensures that the graphics on other states are not overwritten.

10 Make sure Current State Only and Selected Slices Only are selected and that Include Areas Without Slices is *not* selected. Fireworks will export only the current (State 2) version of the racer, and ignore all other areas.

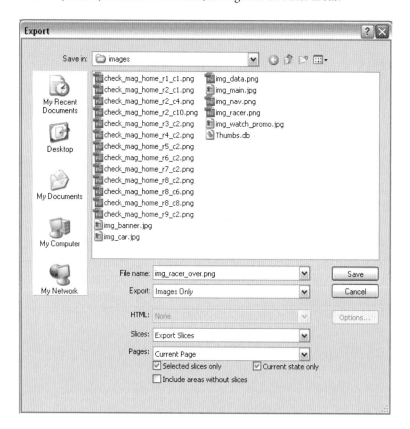

11 Change the filename to **img_racer_over**.

12 Click Save (Windows) or Export (Mac).

Editing the HTML

When you export a single state—as you did in steps 2–5—Fireworks still adds in the JavaScript to create the rollover, but it doesn't add a filename for the rollover image. You need to make one small update to the HTML file in order for the rollover to work.

1 Launch Dreamweaver or your preferred web-page editor. For the purposes of this exercise, we'll assume you are using Dreamweaver.

2 Open the web-page (check_mag_home.htm).

3 Switch to Code View.

4 Scroll down to line 80 and locate this bit of code: **'images/.png'**.

5 Change the code to **'images/img_racer_over.png'**.

6 Save the file. You can test the rollover right in Dreamweaver CS4 or CS5 by clicking the Live View button, or simply open the file from within your web browser.

7 Quit Dreamweaver and your browser, and then save and close the design file in Fireworks.

About Fireworks and CSS

CSS (Cascading Style Sheets) is the current standard for web-page design, and Fireworks has an export workflow to help you in this regard as well. Bear in mind that this doesn't exempt you from learning and understanding how to use CSS in your web-page layouts! It is meant as a starting point to producing a more usable web-page right from Fireworks. Typically, even after exporting in this manner, you will want to do some customizing in your web-page editor.

Here you will learn how to export a CSS-based layout, but we won't be discussing the fine details of Cascading Style Sheets. Entire books have been written on CSS and its use, and this book does not pretend to be one of them. To begin with, we're going to give you a lot of preparatory information, explaining the logic behind the CSS and Images export feature. If you want to just try exporting, you can skip down to the next section, "Exporting CSS and images."

Here are some design concepts to keep in mind if you plan to export a CSS-based layout from Fireworks:

- **Keep it simple.** Overlapping slices will cause Fireworks to export a complete, absolutely positioned layout. While still HTML and CSS valid, it is generally not good practice to produce layouts that are based entirely on absolute positioning.

- **Only text, rectangles, and image slices are exported.** To export as CSS and images, any images you want to include in the web-page must be sliced. Any text you wish to remain as true HTML text should not be sliced. Fireworks creates an HTML web page, using DIV tags to contain the text and images, according to the slices, rectangles, and text it finds in the design. A Cascading Style Sheet is also created, to handle positioning of the DIVs and styling of the text.

- **Text, rectangles, and image slices are all treated as rectangular blocks.** The exporter (also called the export engine) examines the size of text blocks (the actual bounding box, remember, not the width/height of the text itself), rectangles, and slices in order to create the proper spacing between the elements. It also determines the logical placement of columns and rows, based on the position of the design elements in your file.

  Text blocks can be deceiving, because the rectangle area that defines the text block may actually be much larger than the text, causing two objects to overlap, as seen here.

- **The exporter must be able to interpret where the columns and rows of objects exist.** Even though you are not using tables for layout, keep thinking in that grid-like fashion. Make it easy for the export engine to figure out where logical containers—such as a header, a sidebar, a main content area, and a footer—would go.

What is a DIV tag?

The HTML DIV tag is used for defining a section of your document. It acts as a container for other elements of a web page. With the DIV tag, you can group HTML elements together and format them with CSS. For example, you could have your header section, navigation section, and main content sections wrapped in their own separate DIVs.

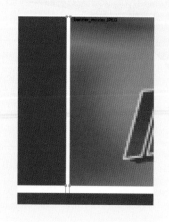

Fireworks wraps text and images inside DIV tags based on the layout, which is why the placement of design elements is critical when exporting in CSS and Images format. In order for Fireworks to lay out the page using its CSS layout engine, it is important that slices do not overlap other slices, and that text areas do not overlap slices.

- **Use rectangles to create a specific DIV around objects.** If you draw a rectangle around specific elements, Fireworks understands that the objects inside the rectangle should be in their own DIV container in the final CSS layout. For example, if you wanted to guarantee that each of the lower columns in the check_mag_home_working.fw.png file were given their own DIV containers in the final layout, you could draw a rectangle around each column. This helps the exporter decide what to do. In the following illustration, we've drawn a rectangle around the left column. Notice how all bounding boxes of the design elements in the column are *inside* the large rectangle. There are no overlaps.

Note: We left the stroke black so you can discern the rectangle from all the other selected objects. If you were to export this file, Fireworks would respect the stroke and create a CSS border around the column. Remove the strokes from rectangles unless you want the border to show up in your web page.

If Fireworks encounters any overlaps, a warning message appears, telling you where the first overlap was encountered and that the export is switching to Absolute Positioning mode. This mode is still CSS-based, but Fireworks places each object at an exact location in the web page—the elements in the page are fixed in place. If you later wish to add text in a web-page editor, or other content using a content-management system, or if a user increases the size of the text for better readability, the other page elements won't shift to accommodate the extra space needed.

Note: For more information on the CSS Export feature, be sure to check out the Adobe Fireworks Developer Center at www.adobe.com/devnet/fireworks/.

The CSS and Images export feature does not export rollover graphics or hotspot information. Hyperlinks are maintained for foreground images, though Fireworks displays a warning message to remind you of that fact. Image maps or JavaScript behaviors need to be added in a web-page editor. On the bright side, you would get to practice creating CSS-based rollovers!

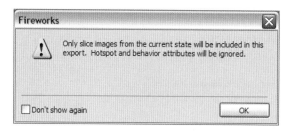

Preparing for CSS and images export

You will test the CSS and Images export using the same file you've been working with (check_mag_home_start.fw.png). If you prefer, you can skip to the exercise, "Exporting CSS and images," and use the prepared file, check_mag_home_css_finished.fw.png, which has all the slicing and prep work done for you. (Hint: You'll learn more if you keep working with your own file).

Tip: To check for overlaps in your design, press Command+A (Mac) or Ctrl+A (Windows) to select all the objects in the design. This will show you if any bounding boxes (text or graphics) are colliding.

1   Press Command+0 (Mac) or Ctrl+0 (Windows) so that you can see the entire design. Notice the layout is grid-like. There are distinct gaps between the various content areas. Although these gaps are not necessary for a successful CSS and Images export, they make it easier for someone new to the feature to understand what is going on. The important thing to remember is to avoid overlaps between slices, rectangles, or text.

The basic structure of web pages is, essentially, some sort of grid. Sometimes that grid is not very obvious and sometimes there are objects in DIV containers that sit *above* the main page layout (such as a pop-up slideshow or a SWF file), but these are in addition to the basic page structure.

2   Select the img_nav slice. In the Properties panel, notice that the Type field says Foreground Image.

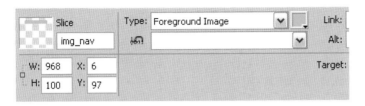

For CSS and Images export, you can set three different types of slices:

- **Foreground Image**—Sets the images in the web-page to be inline images, which are part of the flow of the document. This is the default slice type.

- **Background Image**—When this type is selected, you can set other CSS-related attributes for background images, such as repeat, scroll, vertical position, and horizontal position. A background image is referenced in the style sheet and is not part of the HTML page itself.

- **HTML**—Allows you to add true HTML code to a slice, rather than just an image. This slice type does not work with the CSS and Images export; it works only when exporting HTML.

All the slices in this file are Foreground Image slices, but you will be changing that.

3   Change the img_nav slice type to Background Image.

4   In the Layers panel, expand the navigation layer, and hide the sublayer called text. If the text remains visible in the slice, it will be exported as part of the graphic. Because this slice will become a background image, it cannot have HTML links applied to it.

Most important, in a CSS layout, best practices call for these links to be created using HTML text, usually formatted as an unordered list and styled accordingly. As this navigation sits within a sliced image area, creating the navigation is not a job for Fireworks, and the navigation menu would need to be created later in a web-page editor.

5   Save your file as check_mag_home_css_working.fw.png.

▶ **Tip:** In the HTML section of the Common Library panel, there are two component symbols: Link and List Item. These component symbols can be used to created text-based links that will export as true HTML text, as long as there are no slices covering the text. To learn more about component symbols, refer to Fireworks help and to this excellent article by Matt Stow: www.adobe.com/devnet/fireworks/articles/standards_compliant_design.html.

● **Note:** For the HTML and Images export option, you can choose between foreground image or HTML. Choosing Background image still exports the file as an inline image within a table cell.

Creating your own DIV containers

To ensure that the three columns at the bottom of the page remain as three unique columns, you will use rectangles to identify the DIVs.

1 Select the Background layer.

2 Use the Zoom tool to zoom in on the first column.

3 Select the Rectangle tool from the Vector tools and draw a box around the heading, image, and text in column 1.

4 In the Properties panel, set Fill Color to None, Stroke Color to Black, Size to 1 Pixel, and Stroke Category to Basic > Hard Line.

5 Set the width of the rectangle to 318 pixels, the height to 322 pixels, X to 5 pixels, and Y to 581 pixels. This ensures that the rectangle border does not overlap the header, image, or text edges. You can check this yourself by holding Shift and clicking on the three objects.

6 In the Layers panel, rename this rectangle **col1**.

▶ **Tip:** Feel free to hide other layers (from the Layers panel) if doing so makes it easier to add the DIV rectangles.

7 Create two more rectangles, either by copying and pasting, or by drawing with the rectangle tool, and place them over the other two columns. Their coordinates should be: col2 X position of 331 and col3 X position of 657. It's important that none of the three rectangles overlap each other.

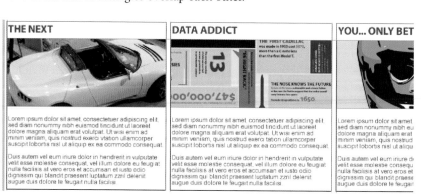

8   Rename the rectangles **col2** and **col3**, respectively. These names will become the ID names for each column DIV tag.

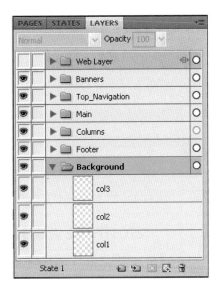

9   Set the stroke color for each rectangle to None. If the stroke is left visible, Fireworks will generate CSS border code for each rectangle, and the design doesn't call for borders around each column.

10   Save your file.

Exporting CSS and images

You're now ready to export the design.

1   Choose File > Export, and browse to the Lesson08 folder.

2   Create a new folder called **csswebpage** and name your file check_mag_home_css.

3   Choose CSS And Images from the Export menu in the Export dialog box.

4   Make sure the Put Images In Subfolder option is selected. The path to this folder should be the new "csswebpage" folder you just created. If it looks like Fireworks is pointing to another images folder (such as the one from the last export), click the Browse button and create an images folder in the proper location.

5   Click the Options button.

     For CSS export, the General tab is the only one you need to concern yourself with. You can tell Fireworks to write the CSS to a separate file, choose an existing image to set as a background image, and set the page alignment.

6   Ensure that Write CSS To An External File is selected.

7 Make sure the Page Alignment field is set to Center.

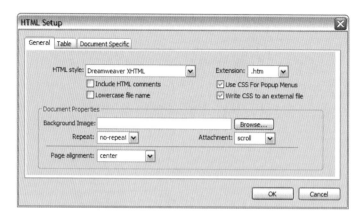

8 Click OK, and then click Save (Windows) or Export (Mac).

A warning box appears, telling you this file uses nonstandard web fonts, and recommends that you either a) add a slice over that text to export it as a graphic or b) cancel the operation and change the fonts to more common ones.

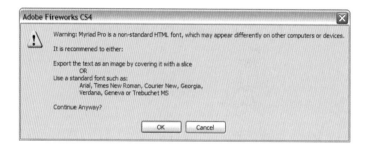

This is important to note. Web browsers rely on the user's fonts for displaying text on a page, so if you have chosen an unusual font, the person visiting your site may not see what you had intended. Instead, they may end up with Arial, Helvetica, Times New Roman, or some other more common font.

This time, though, by agreeing to use whatever nonstandard fonts you like, you will laugh in the face of the World Wide Web. Well, maybe a quiet chuckle will do.

9 Click OK to continue with the export.

Viewing the page

You're now ready to view the page in a web browser.

1 Open the csswebpage folder in Windows Explorer or the Finder.

The folder contains check_mag_home_css.htm (or check_mag_home.html if you changed the file extension preferences), check_mag_home.css, and the images folder containing seven images.

2 Double-click on the web-page to open it in a web browser.

▶ **Tip:** To learn more about which fonts are safe to use on the Web, check out Code Style's Most Common Fonts survey results at www. codestyle.org/css/ font-family/sampler-CombinedResults.shtml.

The page opens, centered in the browser window. Other than that, it seems pretty much like the HTML export. Or is it?

3 Run your mouse over the racer image. No image rollover occurs. When you export as CSS and images, any JavaScript behaviors—such as image rollovers—are ignored. Additional states are also ignored. In your web-page editor, you can work with CSS to generate the rollover image.

4 Notice that the navigation slice has no text links. Again, creating your navigation as HTML text would need to be done in your web-page editor.

5 Scroll down to the bottom of the page, and try again to select the text. This time you *can*. The CSS Export script has recognized these unsliced areas as text and has exported them as such. Even the blue headings have been exported as text.

If you were to open the page in Dreamweaver and select the text, you would see that the text is within paragraph tags. Each column is surrounded by a DIV with an ID name based on the rectangles you created in Fireworks.

6 Save and close the file in Fireworks.

Review questions

1 Why should images be optimized for the web?

2 What are the two types of web objects you can create in a Fireworks design, and how do they differ?

3 How do you create an image slice?

4 What are the main workflows for generating web pages from Fireworks?

Review answers

1 Optimizing graphics ensures that they are set to a suitable format and possess the right balance of file size, color, file compression, and quality. You are trying to get the smallest possible file size (for quick downloads) while maintaining acceptable quality in the image. Optimizing graphics in Fireworks involves choosing the best file format for a graphic and setting format-specific options, such as color depth or quality level.

2 Slices and hotspots are the two main kinds of web objects you can create in Fireworks. Both types of web objects can have URLs added to them for interactivity.

Slices let you cut up a larger design into smaller pieces and individually optimize each slice to get the most suitable combination of file size and image quality. Slices can also be used to generate rollover effects.

Hotspots create an interactive area within an image. They do not cut up an image like slices do. They were commonly used to create image maps—a single image that had multiple hyperlinks applied to it in different areas of the image. Hotspots can also be used to trigger rollover events on the web page.

3 You can create an image slice in one of two ways:

- You can right-click (or Control-click) an object in your design, and then choose Insert Rectangular Slice.

- Using the Slice tool, you can manually draw a slice on top of an object or objects within the design.

4 There are two main workflows for exporting complete HTML pages:

- **File > Export > HTML and Images.** This exports rigid, table-based design consisting entirely of graphics. Even the text is exported as graphics. Pages created this way are difficult to edit, because removing or adding new elements to them using a web-page editor can break the layout. However, this export is ideal for creating interactive prototypes of a web page or a website. While not suitable for a final website, the HTML pages can show the client how the site will look, and can also support rollovers and hyperlinks, so a client can interact with the prototype and request changes or approve a design before any work needs to be done on the coding side of the project.

- **File > Export > CSS and Images.** This option can generate a more standards-based, editable web-page by creating the layout using Cascading Style Sheets rather than tables. Moreover, this export option recognizes text, and exports it as true HTML text. With a working knowledge of CSS, these pages are easier to edit and more flexible in terms of adding new elements within a web-page editor.

9 USING SYMBOLS

Lesson overview

Symbols are one of the great time-saving features in Fireworks. They've been around since the beginning of the application. Symbols can contain multiple objects within a single asset while still giving you quick access to editing those objects. They are a great option for reusing common graphical elements in a design—like a logo or a button. Symbols can contain text, vectors, and bitmaps, each with its own Live Filter attributes.

In this lesson, you'll learn how to do the following:

- Create and edit a graphic symbol

- Create and edit an animation symbol

- Create and edit a button symbol

- Save a symbol to the common library

 This lesson takes approximately 60 minutes to complete. Copy the Lesson09 folder into the Lessons folder that you created on your hard drive for these projects (or create it now, if you haven't already done so). As you work on this lesson, you won't preserve the start files. If you need to restore the start files, copy them from the *Adobe Fireworks CS5 Classroom in a Book* CD.

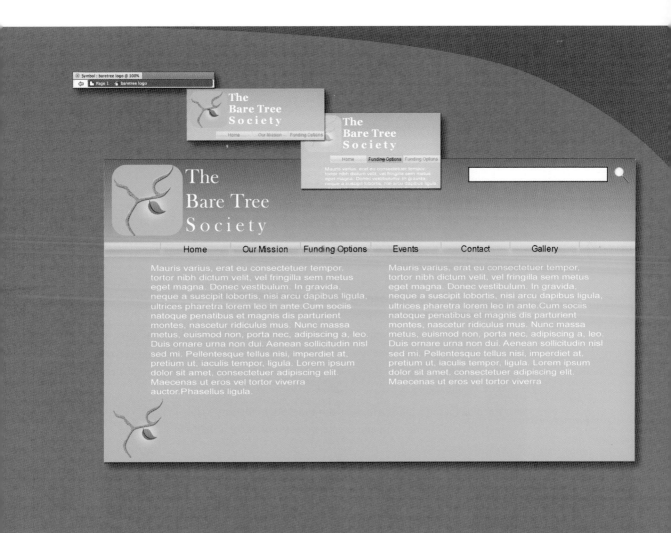

Symbols are great to reuse and share common graphical elements in a design—like a logo or a button.

What are symbols?

A symbol is a master version of a graphic or of a collection of graphics.

A symbol is essentially a self-contained document within a document. You have all the editing capabilities at your fingertips that you would have for a complete design, but all the assets of the symbol itself are kept together.

When you place a symbol on the canvas, you're actually placing a linked copy of the symbol, which is known as an *instance*. When you edit the original symbol object, the linked instances on the canvas automatically change to reflect the edited symbol.

You can also edit any symbol instance on the canvas, changing size, color, or opacity, or adding Live Filters, without altering the original symbol. For example, you might have a fairly large image of a company logo. If you convert that image into a symbol, you can simply drag an instance onto the canvas and scale it down without affecting the quality or size of the original large version.

Another advantage to symbols is increased productivity. Instead of having to locate the original file each time you need a logo, you can turn it into a symbol and make it quickly available from the Document Library panel. This is a big advantage if you regularly reuse objects.

Although you can build your own, Fireworks also comes with a wealth of predesigned symbols that you can use as part of your designs or for jump-starting your own creative talents.

Three main types of symbols are available within Fireworks: graphic, button, and animation symbols. There is also an enhanced graphic symbol type referred to as a *component symbol*. In this lesson, you will be creating and editing the three standard symbol types.

You'll be taking a bit of a break from the Double Identity assets in this lesson. Instead, you'll work with and create some symbols for a different web project.

Graphic symbols

A graphic symbol is a commonly used asset in Fireworks. It is a static, single-state symbol that can be used over and over again throughout a document (or other documents as well, depending on how you set it up). Use a graphic symbol if you do not require built-in animation or multiple states.

Creating graphic symbols

In this exercise, you will convert a simple logo graphic into a graphic symbol.

1 Open the file called baretree_logo.fw.png.

2 Make sure rulers and tooltips are active (View > Rulers And View > Tooltips).

3 Press Ctrl+A (Windows) or Command+A (Mac).

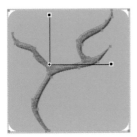

4 Choose Modify > Symbol > Convert To Symbol.

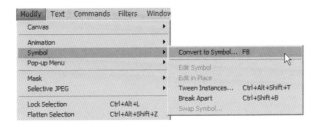

5 Name the symbol **baretree logo**.

6 Make sure Type is set to Graphic, and leave the options deselected.

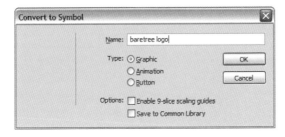

7 Click OK.

8 Open the Document Library panel. The new symbol is displayed there.

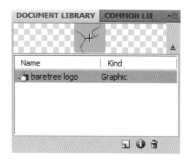

Saving to the Common Library

When creating a new symbol, saving it to the Common Library removes the object from the canvas. You need to locate the newly created symbol in the Custom Symbol folder of the Common Library panel and insert it back into your document.

The advantage to selecting the Save To Common Library option in the Convert To Symbol dialog box is that the new symbol becomes available to *any* document you work on, not just the current document.

You can always add a symbol to the Common Library after it has been created; for details, see the section "The universal Common Library."

⬤ **Note:** Once a symbol is created, you will notice a faint blue plus sign (+) in the middle of the graphic on the canvas. This indicates that the graphic is a copy—or instance—of the symbol.

The universal Common Library

When you create a symbol without adding it to the Common Library, it is linked only to the document where it was created. If you open or create another document, you won't see your newly created symbol in the Document Library. After you have gone to all the trouble of creating those symbols, you may want them available for use in other designs, without having to first open a file, copy the instance on the canvas, and then paste it into a new document. This is where the Common Library comes to the rescue. The Common Library makes symbols easily accessible for any design.

1 In the Document Library panel, select the baretree logo symbol.

2 Choose Save To Common Library from the Document Library panel menu.

A Save As dialog box (or Save dialog box on the Mac) opens, and it should point to the Custom Symbols folder, where all user-created custom common symbols are located by default. This folder displays automatically in the Common Library panel, so it's a good idea to save your new symbol there.

There is a specific structure to symbol file names, starting with the symbol name and appended with the symbol type (graphic, animation, or button), preceded by a period.

3 Click Save.

Adding a graphic symbol to a document

You will now add this graphic symbol to a partially completed web-page design.

1 Open the file simple_page.fw.png from the Lesson09 folder.

2 Open the Common Library panel (Window > Common Library).

3 Choose the Custom Symbols folder. The baretree logo symbol is displayed in the panel.

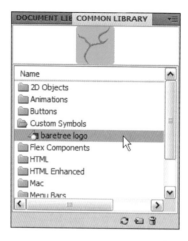

4 Drag the symbol onto the canvas. You now have an instance of the symbol of the canvas—a rather large instance, actually.

5 In the Properties panel, lock the proportions and change the width to **100** pixels, and then press the Tab key to move to the height field. The instance resizes proportionately.

6 Use the Pointer tool to reposition the instance of the logo to the upper-left corner, at a position of X: 10 and Y: 10.

Note: Once a symbol has been copied from the Common Library, it becomes part of that file's Document Library. Dragging the symbol a second time from the Common Library will prompt a warning message from Fireworks stating that one or more library items already exists in the document.

7   If necessary, open the Document Library panel.

Now you'll add another instance of the same symbol, but don't worry—it won't end up looking repetitive.

8   Drag a new instance of the baretree logo from the Document Library panel onto the canvas.

9   In the Properties panel, lock the proportions and change the width to **70** pixels, and then press the Tab key to move to the height field.

10 Select the Pointer tool and drag the object to the lower-left corner, 10 pixels from the right and bottom edges (X: 10, Y: 340).

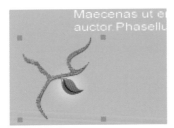

Editing graphic symbols

Some attributes—like size, opacity, blending mode, and Live Filters—can be applied to individual instances on the canvas. Changes to a selected instance do not affect other instances on the canvas. Editing the symbol, however, changes properties in all instances of the symbol.

In this exercise, you're going to add another graphic element to this admittedly rather bare logo.

1   Using the Pointer tool, double-click on the larger of the two baretree instances. Everything but the instance fades slightly, and a breadcrumb bar appears above the document window.

You are now in a symbol-editing mode called Edit In Place mode (a feature that has been available in Adobe Flash for quite some time). You can also enter this mode by choosing Modify > Symbol > Edit In Place. The breadcrumb trail tells you how far you have drilled down into a symbol. Changes made to a symbol in this mode are instantly reflected in all the linked instances on the canvas.

You can exit in-place editing and switch back to the main design by clicking on the top-level breadcrumb (Page 1) or by double-clicking anywhere on the canvas except the active symbol.

2   Choose File > Open and browse for leaf.fw.png. This image comprises three vector objects.

3   Press Ctrl+A (Windows) or Command+A (Mac) to select all the objects.

4   Choose Modify > Group to group the three vectors together. This will make it easier to move and manage the image. You can always ungroup it later, should you need to edit it again.

5   Choose Edit > Copy and return to the simple_page file. You should still be in the Edit In Place symbol-editing mode.

6   Choose Edit > Paste. Note that the smaller instance also updates with the pasted leaf.

7   Zoom in to 200%.

8   In the Properties panel, lock the proportions and resize the leaf to about 25 pixels wide.

9   If you zoom back out, you will see the smaller logo also has the leaf.

10 Reposition the leaf to X: −1, Y: 0. When you are in symbol-editing mode, the X and Y coordinates are relative to the registration point in the center of the symbol.

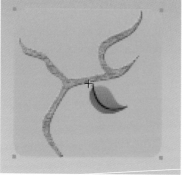

Isolation Mode

Another option for editing symbols is referred to as *isolation mode*. This is the default mode for any symbol to which the 9-Slice Scaling Guides option has been applied. You can access isolation mode for any symbol, though, by choosing Modify > Symbol > Edit Symbol. The symbol remains on the canvas, but all other objects are hidden from view. If you have a full design, this mode may make it easier for you to edit aspects of symbols without any distractions.

11 Click the background rectangle of the logo.

12 In the Properties panel, change the Fill Category to Gradient > Radial. The outer part of the gradient should be the original green fill color; the central part will be black. You need to change the inner color from black to yellow.

13 Click the Fill color box in the Properties panel, and then click the black color swatch in the Gradient pop-up window. Choose a rich yellow (#FFFF00) from the color picker.

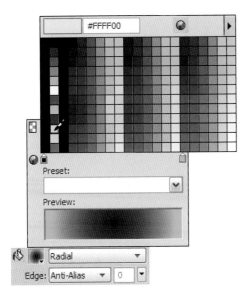

14 Reposition the gradient so that it starts near the center of the leaf.

15 Adjust the length of the gradient so that the rectangle fades to a solid green at the right side, similar to what's shown here.

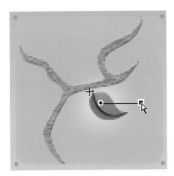

The effect is applied to both instances.

16 Click on Page 1 of the breadcrumb trail to return to the main design.

17 Save the file as **simple_page_working.fw.png**.

Adding prebuilt symbols from the Common Library

Note: The Common Library does not become populated with symbols until a document is open in Fireworks.

The Common Library holds a wealth of prebuilt symbols you can use for your designs or as a starting point for your own symbols. To familiarize yourself with this useful feature, you will add a mockup of a search box using a rectangle and a prebuilt symbol. Make sure you're back on Page 1 in your document.

1   Open the Common Library panel and scroll down until you see the Web & Application folder.

2   Double-click the folder icon (Windows) or click the disclosure triangle (Mac) to open the folder.

3   Locate the Search symbol.

4   Drag the symbol—either the graphic itself or its name—onto the canvas.

The instance of a magnifying glass is fairly large and needs to be resized.

5   Lock the Proportions in the Properties panel and set the width to 20 pixels.

6   Tab to the next field and the instance dimensions update on the canvas.

7 Select the Pointer tool, and reposition the magnifying glass to X: 720, Y: 12.

8 Select the Rectangle tool, and then unlock the proportions in the Properties panel.

9 Draw a rectangle that is 200 pixels wide by 20 pixels high.

10 Fill the rectangle with white, and give it a black, 1-pixel hard stroke.

11 Use the Pointer tool to position the rectangle at X: 510, Y: 12.

12 Save the file.

You now have a mockup of a search bar.

Button symbols

Button symbols serve a specific purpose: making button rollover states for navigation buttons.

Button symbols are an efficient way of generating up to four visible states for a button (Up, Over, Down, and Over While Down) and adding a hyperlink. Almost any graphic or text object can become a button. After you have created a single button symbol, you can reuse it again and again for navigation. Each instance of a button symbol can also have its own custom text label, URL, and target without breaking the two-way symbol–instance relationship.

A button instance is self-contained. The slice object, graphic elements, and states are kept together, so as you move the Up state of a button on the main canvas, the other states and the button slice move with it.

When you export a button using the HTML And Images option, Fireworks generates the JavaScript necessary to display the rollover effect in a web browser. In Adobe Dreamweaver, you can easily insert JavaScript and HTML code from Fireworks into your web pages or into any HTML file (handy for interactive HTML prototypes).

Note: For production sites, most designers tend to create the rollover effect using CSS and background images, rather than JavaScript and inline images. However, button symbols can't be beat for creating interactive HTML prototypes.

Creating button symbols

You can create a button from any object, but usually the button starts out as a vector shape or a bitmap object. Make sure the simple_page.fw.png file is still open.

1 Select the Rectangle tool, and draw a rectangle that is 100 pixels wide by 20 pixels high.

2 Use the Pointer tool or the Properties panel to position the rectangle at X: 80 and Y: 115.

3   Open the Styles panel, and choose Plastic Styles from the Styles list.

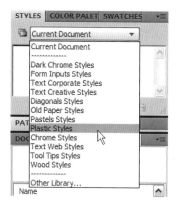

4   Choose the style Plastic 044. The rectangle takes on a glassy, green style.

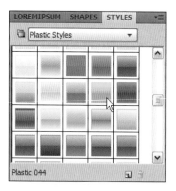

5   Choose Modify > Symbol > Convert To Symbol.

6   Name the symbol **navButton**.

7 Change Type to Button, and click OK.

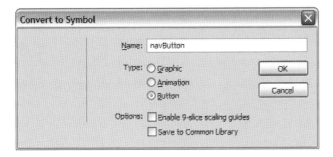

You're now back on the main canvas. Fireworks automatically adds a slice to a button symbol, because button symbols are mainly used for rollover effects, and a slice allows for image swapping to other button states.

To maintain a good-quality gradient, you will set the export options for this file to PNG-24.

8 Open the Optimize panel and, if necessary, choose PNG-24 from the Export File Format list. PNG-24 will do a better job of maintaining crisp text than the JPEG format, and even though PNG files will be larger in file size than JPEGs, the small size of these buttons should not add too much weight to the final page.

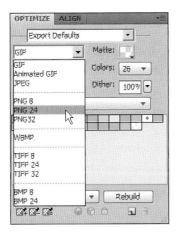

Editing a button symbol

At first, a button symbol (like a graphic symbol) only has one state. Buttons also need text labels. The slice created by Fireworks tries to include all visual properties of the button, some of which are not easy to see. You will add text to the button, and add another state.

1   Double-click the button slice. All objects other than the button are grayed out.

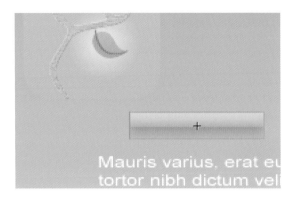

2   Select the Text tool and then in the Properties panel, set the font family to Arial, font style to regular, size to 12 points, Fill Category to Solid, and Color to Black.

3   Set the text alignment to Center Alignment and the anti-aliasing level to No Anti-Alias.

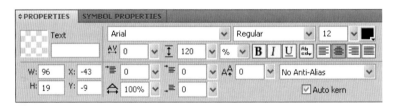

▶ **Tip:** The expectation with button symbols is that you will be creating one or more graphical navigation buttons, with different visual appearances to reflect the state of the button. So it is important to determine what the longest string of button text will be, in order to set a font size that will allow the various button-text strings to fit comfortably within the button shape.

4   Click right on top of the rectangle, and type **Funding Options.**

5   Select the Pointer tool, and drag over both the rectangle and the text block to select them.

6   Open the Align panel, and click the Align horizontal center ( ) and Align vertical center ( ) icons to position the text within the rectangle.

While we're here, let's create a rollover state.

7   Click away from the button using the Pointer tool.

8 In the Properties panel, choose Over from the State menu. The button disappears.

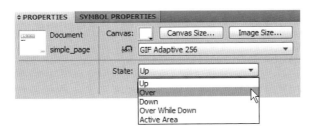

9 Click the Copy Up Graphic button. This adds a duplicate of the Up state to the Over State.

10 Select the rectangle using the Pointer tool.

11 Open the Gradient Editor and choose Reverse Gradients.

12 Select the text block.

13 In the Properties panel, change the font style to Bold and the color to White.

14 Click the Page 1 breadcrumb to go back to the main canvas.

● **Note:** If you only have Faux Bold (rather than the true font style option), you may have to reduce the size of your font by a couple pixels to keep the text inside the button rectangle.

Adding more buttons

Most sites need more than a single navigation button, so you will add a few more.

1   Make sure the Pointer tool is selected and the button slice is active.

2   Hold down the Alt (Windows) or Option (Mac) key, and use the Pointer tool to drag the button to the right, until it snaps to the right edge of the original button. (Holding down Alt/Option creates a copy of the selected object.) Let the Smart Guides help you position the new button directly next to the first button.

3   Select both buttons, and then repeat step 2 twice, so you have six buttons.

All six buttons currently have the same text labels. That's not much help!

4   Select the leftmost button. The words *Funding Options* appear in the text box in the Properties panel.

5   Change the text to **Home**, and press Enter or Return.

The button text updates.

6   Select the second button.

7   Change the button text to **Our Mission**, and press Enter or Return.

8   Skip the third button, as it already says Funding Options.

9   Select the fourth button, and change the text to **Events**.

10 Change the text for the fifth button to **Contact** and the sixth button to **Gallery**.

Take this time to rename the slices as well.

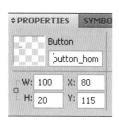

11 Click on the Home button, and in the Properties panel, change the button name to **button_home**.

12 Click on the Our Mission button, and change the button name to **button_mission**.

13 Click on the Funding Options button, and change the button name to **button_funding**.

14 On the subsequent three buttons, change the names to **button_events**, **button_contact**, and **button_gallery**, respectively.

▶ **Tip:** Using a consistent "heading" word for each slice name (such as "button_" in this exercise) makes it easier to find groups of similar graphics in Windows Explorer, the Mac Finder, or even in Dreamweaver's Files panel, as this is the name Fireworks will use when you export the graphics.

Testing rollovers

Now it's time to test the rollovers.

1 Click the Hide Slices And Hotspots icon (▣) in the Tools panel.

2 Click the Preview button at the top of the document window.

3 Move your mouse over the six buttons. On each one, the gradient reverses and the text turns white when you mouse over it.

4 Switch back to Original view.

Completing the design

For a finishing touch on your mockup, you will add some text next to the top logo instance.

1 Select the Text tool.

2 In the Properties panel, choose a conservative serif font. We chose Georgia.

3 Set the font style to Bold.

4 Set the font size to 28 points. This may need some adjustment, depending on your own font selection.

5 Set the Kerning/Tracking value to 20.

6 Set Leading to 110, instead of the default 120.

7 Set the text alignment to Left aligned and the text color to White.

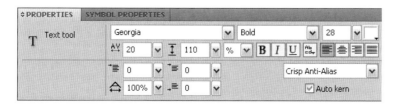

8 Click to the right of the logo at the top of the page, and type **The Bare Tree Society**. Use the Return or Enter key to break the text into three lines.

9 Double-click the word Society to select it.

10 Hold the Shift and Ctrl keys (Shift+Command for Mac) and press the right arrow key twice. This increases the kerning by another 200%.

11 Release the Shift key and press the right arrow key three more times, increasing the kerning by another 30%. At this point, the word Society should stretch to the width of the words just above.

12 Save the file.

With your main page mockup completed, save the file as **simple_page_complete. fw.png**. You will use this file again in the next exercise lessons. You can compare your version to our completed one, simple_page_final.fw.png, if you like.

Animation symbols

Animation symbols let you quickly generate various types of state-based animation, including movement, visibility, opacity, and size. Because animations require multiple states in a document, they are best created on their own—either in a new document or on a separate page of an existing document, rather than as part of a complete web-page design. This eliminates the potential for exporting unwanted images from other parts of the design.

● **Note:** If you need a refresher on the concepts of pages or states, refer back to Lesson 2.

Creating animation symbols

In your sample design, you have a small version of the logo placed at the bottom left of the page. You are going to animate this instance so it enters the page on the left and slides over to the right, reducing in size slightly as it moves across the page. You will do this on a new page of your existing simple_page_complete.fw.png file.

1 Open the Pages panel by clicking the Pages tab in the panel dock.

   If you cannot find the Pages panel, choose Window > Pages.

2 Create a new empty page by clicking the New/Duplicate page icon at the bottom right of the panel.

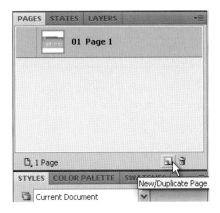

A new, empty page is created, using the same dimensions as the original page. In the Pages panel, you now have Page 1 and Page 2.

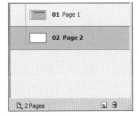

3 In the Properties panel, click the Canvas Size button. Be sure that Current Page Only is selected and change the canvas size of this page to **760** pixels x **140** pixels.

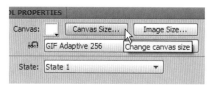

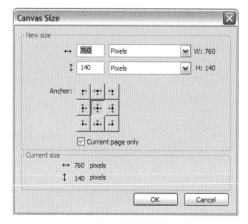

4 In the Properties panel, change the Canvas Color to **#00CC00**.

5 Open the Document Library panel and drag the baretree_logo symbol onto the canvas.

6 In the Properties panel, lock the proportions and change the width to **102** pixels and then tab to the X field.

7 Set X to **16** pixels and then tab to Y and set that value to **20** pixels.

8 Right-click (Windows) or Control-click (Mac) on the instance, and choose Animation > Animate Selection.

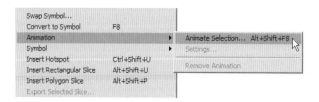

9 Change the following values in the Animate dialog box:

- States: **9**

- Move: **650**

- Scale: **70**

Leave all other fields as they are, and click OK.

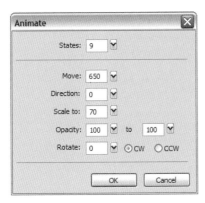

10 A dialog box appears, asking if you want to add additional states to this page. Click OK.

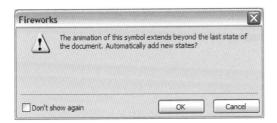

You are returned to the canvas. The logo now has a blue path attached to it, with nine anchor points, representing the position of the nine states of the animation. The starting anchor point is green, and the ending anchor point is red.

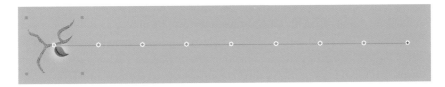

Fireworks has added this instance of the logo as a new symbol in the Document Library panel. It needs a better name.

11 Double-click on the symbol in the Document Library panel to open the Convert To Symbol dialog box, rename the symbol **logo animation**, and click OK.

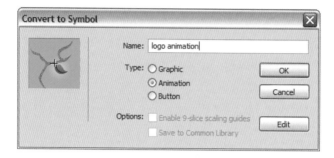

At the bottom of the document window are animation playback controls.

12 Click the Play icon to see the animation.

Note: You have also created a nested symbol by making this animation. Double-clicking on the first frame of the animation instance will bring you to the logo animation symbol. Double-clicking again will bring you to the original baretree logo symbol. Any changes you make to the nested baretree logo will update all instances of the symbol on all pages, whether or not they are part of the animation symbol. To eliminate this potential problem, you can right-click (or Control-click) the nested baretree logo symbol and choose Symbol > Break Apart. This will break the link between the artwork in the animation symbol and the original baretree logo.

Onion skinning

Animation symbols are a bit different from just having objects in different states. The animation direction and distance is controlled by dragging the animation path in State 1. Normally, you see only the objects that are part of a selected state. However, you can use a feature called *onion skinning* to see as many states as you like. Onion skinning allows you to see states that occur before and after the currently selected state.

You are going to adjust the angle of the animation slightly, so the final state is at the same distance from the bottom of the screen as the first state.

1 Making sure rulers are visible (View > Rulers), drag down a guide from the top ruler so it rests at the bottom of the logo.

2 Select the logo on the canvas.

3 If necessary, open the States panel.

4 Choose Show All States from the Onion Skinning (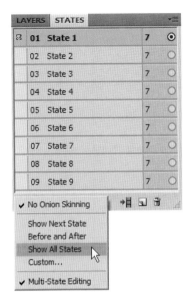) menu at the bottom of the panel.

The canvas now displays each state of the animation.

5 Select the Pointer tool.

6 Click outside the canvas area to show your canvas settings in the Properties panel.

7 Change the Canvas color to white. This will make the next steps easier.

8 Select the first state of the animation. The animation path will reappear.

You need to adjust the animation path so the states line up at the bottom edge, and you will also need to reposition the final state so it is completely within the canvas.

> **Note:** You will also notice a vertical line with start and stop nodes running down the States panel to the left of the state names. This is a visual representation of the onion skinning. You can adjust the onion skinning settings by clicking in the onion-skinning box next to each state name.

9 Click and drag the red anchor point lower and inward to the left so that the last state of the animation rests on the guide you added earlier in the exercise. There is no preview for this process, nor do tooltips or guide snapping work. This will involve a bit of trial and error.

Optimizing the animation

To make this series of states into a true web animation, you must change the format to Animated GIF. First, however, you will trim the canvas to get rid of any unnecessary image data.

1 Choose Modify > Canvas > Trim Canvas. This deletes any excess canvas area from the page.

2 Click outside the canvas area and then reset the canvas color to #00CC00.

3 Select State 1 from the States panel.

4 Open the Optimize panel and choose Animated GIF from the Export File Format menu.

5 Set the number of colors to 256.

6 Set Transparency to Alpha Transparency. This will force the number of colors to 255 in the color input box, because the canvas color is now reserved as a transparent color.

▶ **Tip:** To see changes in the color table, you may have to click the Rebuild button in the Optimize panel.

7 Set Matte color to #00CC00. The matte color helps blend the edges of an anti-aliased bitmap with the background color of the web page.

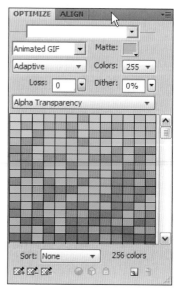

7 Click the 2-Up preview button at the top of the document window.

The first thing you might notice is the glow behind the leaf is no longer a subtle gradation. GIF images support only up to 256 colors. Typically, gradients contain a greater range of hues/tones than that, and this logo is no exception. If you compare the original view to the optimized preview, you will see the gradient in the optimized version is made up of a series of color circles. This "banding" is a result of the GIF's inability to display the full hue range of the gradient.

You will also notice the checkerboard canvas area. This checkerboard indicates a transparent area. By choosing Alpha Transparency in the Optimize panel, Fireworks will export this animated GIF with a see-through canvas area. It also saves us a few bytes in file size.

As for the banding issue, your options are:

- Accept this result

- Switch to a solid-color glow

- Experiment with the optimization settings

For the purposes of this exercise, you will experiment.

The current file size of the GIF image is approximately 20 KB. Ideally, we want to keep the file size no larger than this, but we also want a better-looking gradient.

8 Change the dither setting to **100%**, and compare the images again. A higher dithering percentage creates the appearance of more colors in an image, but can also increase the file size.

9 Again, if a button labeled Rebuild appears in the Optimize panel, click it to rebuild the color table for the document.

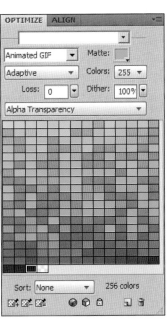

The gradient looks only slightly better now, but this file has increased in size to about 24 KB.

You need to walk the balance between image quality and file size. The process of optimization has already been explained in great detail in Lesson 8, so in this case we will simply make suggestions here. As always, you are welcome to experiment further.

10 Change the number of colors to **32**. There is a noticeable drop in file size. And, odd as it may seem, the glow seems to have slightly less banding in it.

Note: You may see slight variances in file size compared to our numbers, depending on whether you are running Fireworks on Windows or on a Mac. Fireworks on the Mac tends to compress files slightly better.

Now, 32 colors isn't bad, but you should be able to squeeze a bit more out of this file. Time to split some hairs. Aside from the preset color settings, you can also type in your own value for the number of colors.

11 In the Optimize panel, select number 32, and type in **28**. This gives us a file size of about 14 KB. The banding is even less noticeable. The reason for this is that due to the reduced number of colors, the dithering is being applied more heavily. Overall image quality has also been somewhat reduced, but as this will be an animation, the change should not be too noticeable.

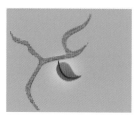 

12 Switch back to the Original view by clicking the Original button.

13 Save the file.

Other ways to reduce file size

You can reduce the file size of a GIF animation in a few different ways:

- Reduce the number of colors used, as demonstrated earlier.
- Reduce the dimensions of the animation.
- Remove states from an animation. The number of states in a GIF animation plays a big role in the final file size. By reducing the number of states to the barest minimum needed, you can significantly reduce the final file size.
- As with objects or layers, to delete a state, simply drag it to the Delete State button in the States panel.

Altering animation settings

Although you can use the playback controls to watch the animation, they do not emulate the true speed of the animation. For this, you will have to preview the animation in a web browser or in the Preview window.

The speed at which the animation runs is referred to as "state delay," and by default, each state in an animation remains visible for 7/100 of a second. Increasing this value (to 20/100s, for example) will slow the animation; conversely, decreasing the value will speed up the animation. You can change the state delay for any individually selected state, or you can select a series of states and alter the delay for all of them.

1 Click the Preview button at the top of the document window.

2 Click the Play icon in the playback controls at the bottom of the document window. Click the Stop icon once the animation has run a couple of times.

3 If necessary, open the States panel.

4 In the States panel, click State 1.

5 Hold the Shift key, and then click State 9.

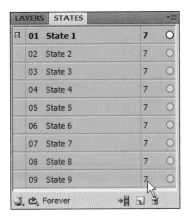

6 Double-click on any of the number 7s that appear to the right of a state name. The State properties box appears.

7 Change the value to **20**, and press Enter or Return. All the states are now set to 20/100 of a second.

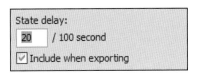

8 Click the Play icon again. The animation plays at a much slower pace.

9 Select all the states again, change the delay to **4/100**, and press Enter or Return.

10 Click the Play icon again. The animation plays much faster.

11 Reset the delay value to **7**.

You can also preview the animation in a web browser by choosing File > Preview In Browser and selecting your preferred web browser. Your playback experience may vary between the browser and the Preview window in Fireworks; as with any web-destined artwork, you should always view your work in as many browsers as you have available.

Note: Regardless of the looping setting you choose, Fireworks will always loop the animation when you click the Play icon in the document window. To test looping, you will have to preview in a browser.

Note: Animated GIFs don't have a lot of features when it comes to animation, which is why you don't see a lot of fancy special options for animation in Fireworks. If you are interested in creating complex animations for the Web, it would be a good idea for you to investigate Adobe Flash.

Looping controls how many times an animation repeats. The default looping value is Forever. That may be useful for some generic animated graphics, but it can also be quite annoying visually.

12 In the States panel, click the Looping icon ( ), and change the value from Forever to No Looping. This forces the exported animation to run once only, and stop.

13 Save the file one more time.

Exporting the animation

You're now ready to export the file as an animated GIF.

1 Choose File > Export.

2 Browse to the Lesson09 folder.

3 Change the name to **logo_animation.**

4 Choose Images Only for the Export type.

5 Set Slices to None, if necessary.

6 Click Save (Windows) or Export (Mac). Feel free to launch a browser and open the GIF animation from the browser's File menu or drag the file onto the page of an already open browser.

Review questions

1   What are the three main types of symbols?

2   What objects can be included in a symbol?

3   How do you create a graphic symbol?

4   What is one way to create an animation symbol?

5   What is the importance of the Common Library?

Review answers

1   The three main types of symbols are graphic symbols, button symbols, and animation symbols.

2   A symbol can include vector, bitmap, or text objects. You can even include other symbols in a symbol, which is referred to *nesting symbols*.

3   To create a graphic symbol, select the objects you wish to be part of the symbol, and then choose Modify > Symbol > Convert To Symbol. Name the symbol in the Convert To Symbol dialog box, and set Type to Graphic. Based on your requirements for this symbol, you can choose to select the Enable 9-slice Scaling and Save To Common Library options.

4   You can create an animation symbol by right-clicking on an object on the canvas and choosing Animation > Animate Selection. In the Animate dialog box you can change properties such as the number of states for the animation, its direction, movement, opacity, size, and rotation.

5   The Common Library contains a large number of prebuilt graphic, button, animation, and component symbols that you can easily drag and drop into your design. You can also save your own custom symbols to the Common Library, so they can be used in any of your documents.

10 PROTOTYPING BASICS

Lesson overview

Layout features (smart guides and tooltips) and the ability to switch seamlessly from vector to bitmap graphic editing make Fireworks an ideal application for building prototypes.

In this lesson, you'll learn how to do the following:

- Edit a multipage wireframe

- Share layers to multiple pages

- Add a button symbol

- Preview a wireframe design in a web browser

- Export a secure, interactive PDF file

This lesson will take about 60 minutes to complete. Copy the Lesson10 folder into the Lessons folder that you created on your hard drive for these projects (or create it now), if you haven't already done so. As you work on this lesson, you won't preserve the start files. If you need to restore the start files, copy them from the *Adobe Fireworks CS5 Classroom in a Book* CD.

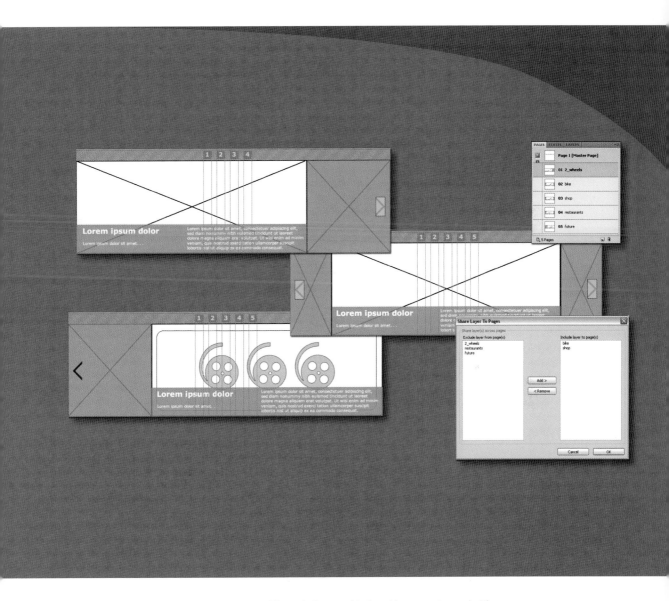

Fireworks is a graphical, rapid-prototyping tool with a multitude of features, such as the Pages panel, interactive Web layers, and component symbols, making it an ideal application for building prototypes to test user interaction and nail down interface or page design issues.

The prototyping workflow

Web-page design, game design, mobile, and application design projects can all benefit from adopting some form of prototyping workflow. Developing a prototype is a good way to maintain design consistency, minimize project creep, and test functionality and design concepts before moving to the coding stage.

A typical prototyping workflow would include:

- Creating a project concept (website, mobile application, game, etc.)
- Creating a wireframe to plan the application layout and functionality
- Creating a realistic prototype to address the aesthetic concerns of the project
- Generating an interactive prototype for "proof of concept" and/or usability testing
- Upon approval, building the final project

This is a simplified description and a workflow may very well require several wireframes and numerous design concepts before a project reaches the realistic prototype stage.

In this lesson you will be working with a wireframe. A wireframe is a simplistic rendition of the final project. The idea behind a wireframe is that it can be quickly built and just as easily discarded when it has served its purpose. The goal of a wireframe is to describe an application's function, flow, and general layout, without focusing on the aesthetics of the application.

Exploring the Pages panel

In Lesson 2, you learned the basics about the Pages feature. As you added content to a simple mockup in that lesson, you learned that pages are a key prototyping strength in Fireworks. The ability to create multiple pages in a single Fireworks file makes it a great tool for creating rich, realistic multipage mockups. With multiple pages, you can easily generate a series of design concepts, an entire website mockup, or an application design in one location, making it easier to keep track of assets for a specific project.

The Pages panel is the control center for adding, duplicating, deleting, and renaming pages.

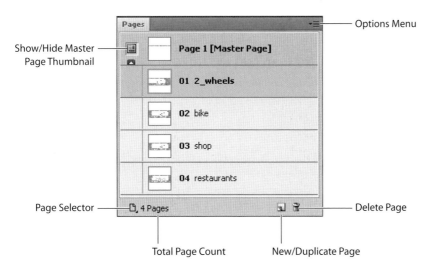

Options Menu

Show/Hide Master Page Thumbnail

Page 1 [Master Page]

01 2_wheels

02 bike

03 shop

04 restaurants

Page Selector — 4 Pages — Delete Page

Total Page Count   New/Duplicate Page

Each page in a document has a sequence number automatically applied by Fireworks. This numbering can be turned on or off from the Pages options menu. You can rename any page just as you can rename layers and objects; simply double-click on the page name to edit it. If your design uses a master page for common page elements, that master page will always appear at the top of the Pages panel.

Isolating the Pages panel

Typically, the Pages panel is grouped with the Layers and States panels, but we find it more useful to move it into its own group. You will do that now.

1   Open the Pages panel (Window > Pages).

2   Hold down the left mouse button on the Pages tab, and reposition the cursor so that it is between any two groups.

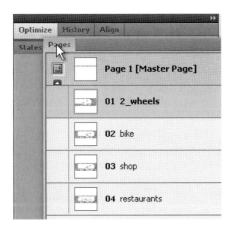

3 When a thin blue highlight bar appears and the panel's opacity fades, release the mouse button. The Pages panel is now in its own group.

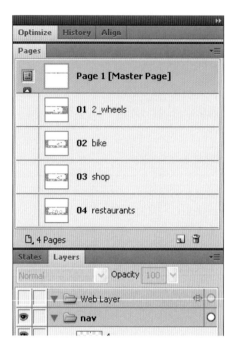

Master pages

The master page is an optional but useful item. Use it if you have visual elements or web objects that will be common to all pages, and in the same physical location on each page. Because each page can have different dimensions, it's best to use a master page only for elements that appear at the top of a design or share a common canvas color. If you are positive your page dimensions will not change, you can also include common background images or footer information in a master page; just bear in mind that if you shorten or lengthen a page, that information may not appear in the correct position.

Each Fireworks design can contain only a single master page.

1 Choose File > Open, and open the local_banner_wireframe.fw.png file.

This is the almost-complete wireframe for a new interactive project. Your goal is to complete the wireframe and turn it into an interactive PDF for client review.

2 Select the master page in this wireframe. Just the navigation elements are present. You may also notice slices on top of the buttons. These buttons are actually button symbols. Using button symbols makes it easy to use the same object for all navigation but still have unique labels for each object. In this case, the buttons have been labeled 1–4.

3 Double-click on the page name.

Change the name to **common**.

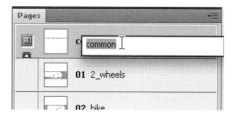

Note: While you can change the name of the master page, the identifier—[Master Page]—cannot be removed or edited.

Comparing wireframe pages

By their nature, wireframes are supposed to be simple diagrams, designed to focus on function and not aesthetics.

1 Select the 2_wheels page. The canvas is filled with simple shapes, and many of these shapes have been converted to symbols to make it easy to build more wireframe pages. Color issues for the final design have been deferred by using shades of gray for all the objects in the wireframe. This way, a client is not focusing on color, hue, or saturation; they are focusing on the functionality of the concept.

Note: While this wireframe is making use of some custom symbols created for the project, you are welcome to use the vector tools to create your own shapes, or build on the knowledge you gained in Lesson 9 to create your own symbols.

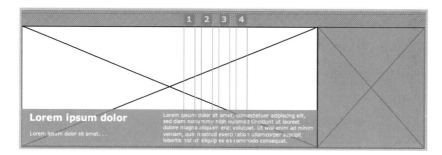

This page contains three main layers, plus the master page layer. Although you can see the master page elements, they cannot be selected or edited from any page but the master page.

2 Select the bike page.

3 Expand the Layers panel. All three main layers have a small page icon appearing near the right side of the layer. This icon indicates that these layers are shared with other pages in the design—another timesaving feature.

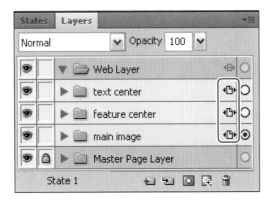

4 Switch to the shop page. It's identical to the bike page on the canvas.

5 Using the Pointer tool, select the large heading text at the left side of the wireframe.

6 Hold down the Shift key and press the Up arrow twice to reposition the text block higher.

7 Switch back to the bike page. The heading text has been repositioned on this page as well. That's the power of a shared layer; you can edit it on any page where it is shared, and the changes propagate across all the sharing pages.

8 Switch to the restaurants page. Its layer hierarchy is similar to the bike and shop pages, but the main image is not a big box with an X through it. The main image on this page has film canisters running through it, symbolizing a video or movie segment, rather than a still image.

On this page, there is no shared main image layer. As with the 2_wheels page, the main image layer on the restaurants page is unique to that specific page. The ability to share layers across specific pages gives you far more control and flexibility than the Master page. The beauty of this feature is that you are in control.

Adding a page

The most expedient way to add more pages to any design is to create a duplicate of another page, if that page is similar in layout. If you have no similar pages, then creating a standard new page is the way to go. You will add one final page to the wireframe, and then use a combination of techniques to flesh it out.

1 Select the restaurants page.

2 At the bottom of the Pages panel, click the Add/Duplicate page icon. Do not drag the restaurants page to this icon; you don't need a copy of that specific page.

3 Save your work.

The new page only displays the content from the master page.

4 Rename the page **future**.

5 Create two more layers in the Layers panel. This makes for a total of three layers.

6 Name the layers **feature left, text,** and **main image** in descending order.

7 Lock the text and feature layers.

8 Open the Document Library and drag the video symbol onto the canvas.

9 Set the X position to 253 pixels and the Y position to 35 pixels.

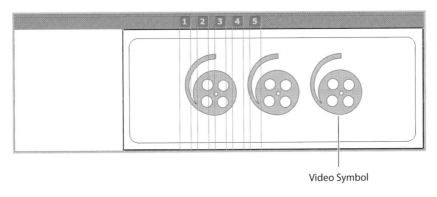

Video Symbol

10 Lock the main image layer and then unlock the feature left layer.

Adding to the feature layer

The main image layer was pretty easy. You'll be working a bit harder on the feature layer.

1 Drag the photo box symbol onto the canvas. This instance will be too small and will require scaling.

2 In the Properties panel, make sure the proportions are not locked; then set the width to 253 pixels and the height to 275 pixels.

3 Set the X value to 0 pixels and the Y value to 35 pixels.

4 Drag the overlay symbol onto the canvas.

5 Scale and position the overlay symbol using the same settings as the photo box.

6 Drag in one more instance of the overlay and set X to 253 pixels and Y to 224 pixels. The dimensions of the instance are fine as they are.

7 Drag the left nav symbol onto the canvas and place it at X: 13 pixels and Y: 144 pixels to complete the work on this layer.

8 Lock the feature layer and unlock the text layer.

Adding content to the text layer

Text needs to go here, obviously, but there's no need to create it from scratch.

1 Select the 2_wheels page.

2 While pressing the Shift key, select the three text objects on the canvas.

3 Press Ctrl+C (Windows) or Command+C (Mac) to copy the objects.

4 Select the future page, and then select the text layer.

5 Paste the objects by pressing Ctrl+V or Command+V.

6 Change the X value to 267 pixels to place the text in the correct location.

7 Save your work.

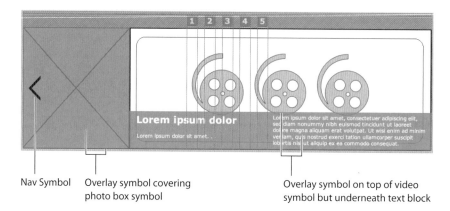

Nav Symbol Overlay symbol covering photo box symbol

Overlay symbol on top of video symbol but underneath text block

Completing the interactivity

The final step is to add the link to the new page.

1 Select the master page.

2 Select button 4 on the canvas. This is a button symbol.

3 Press the Alt key (Windows) or the Option key (Mac) and tap the right arrow key once. This creates a slightly offset duplicate of button 4.

4 In the Properties panel, set the X coordinate to 549 pixels.

5 Change the Button name and Text field values in the Properties panel from 4 to **5**.

6 From the Link drop-down menu, select the newly created page, future.htm.

7 Select the future page in the Pages panel.

8 Right-click (Windows) or Control-click (Mac) the left nav object on the canvas and, from the context menu, choose Insert Hotspot.

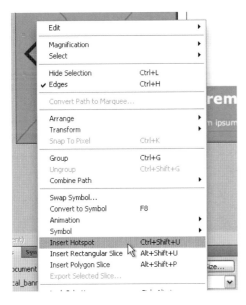

9 In the Properties panel, set the link to restaurants.

10 Save the file.

11 Select File > Preview in Browser > Preview All Pages In to test the wireframe. You should be able to navigate from page to page using either the buttons or the directional arrows in the wireframe.

12 Close the browser when you're done and return to Fireworks.

Delivering the wireframe

Now that the wireframe is complete, it needs to be sent to the client for feedback and/or approval. Fireworks gives you several methods for delivering designs and concepts to a client, but two of them are ideally suited for interactive wireframes: PDF or HTML And Images.

Interactive PDF files enable the client to review the file offline and allow for direct feedback via Acrobat's commenting feature. Links placed on rectangular slices or hotspots are also supported, so the client can browse through the pages using the wireframe's built-in interactivity. Rollover effects, however, are not supported. But for a wireframe, this isn't a huge concern. Rollover effects can be dealt with in the prototyping stage. PDF files can also be password protected.

HTML And Images export supports hyperlinks, rollovers, and any shape of hotspot or slice, but there is no direct feedback mechanism. The wireframe must also be uploaded and viewed online, or delivered on a CD or a flash drive for offline viewing.

Which you choose is up to you. For our simple wireframe, let's export it as a secure, interactive PDF.

Exporting the wireframe

You create a PDF file from Fireworks by exporting the file. But in this case, you only want to export the actual wireframe pages, excluding the master page.

1 In the Pages panel, select 2_wheels.

2 Hold down Shift and then select the future page. All the main pages of the wireframe are now selected.

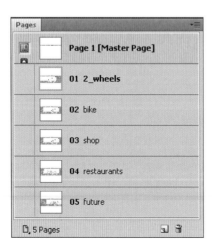

3 Select File > Export.

4 In the Export dialog box, choose a suitable folder location and file name.

5 Change the Export type to Adobe PDF.

6 From the Pages menu, choose Selected Pages.

7 Make sure the View PDF After Export option is selected if you have Acrobat Reader or Acrobat Professional installed. Opening the PDF is the only indication that Fireworks has completed the export.

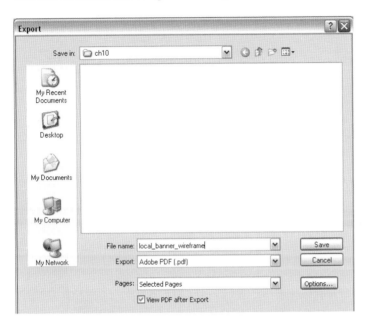

8 Click the Options button.

9 Select the Convert To Grayscale option. This reduces the size of the file slightly, and considering the wireframe is all shades of gray anyway, you won't be compromising the image quality.

10 Select the Use Password To Open Document option and type in the password **test**.

11 Click OK to return to the main Export dialog box, and then click Save (Windows) or Export (Mac).

When the PDF file has been exported, Acrobat Professional—if installed—will launch, allowing you to test the PDF and enable commenting—after you've input the correct password.

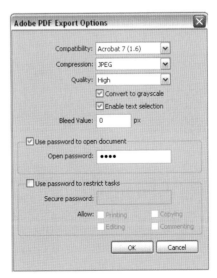

Note: You can also password-protect specific tasks. If you choose to password-protect any of the listed tasks, you must create a different password from the one used to open the document.

Note: If you do not have Acrobat Professional, your default PDF reader will launch. Although you won't be able to enable commenting in the reader, you will be able to view the file once you've entered the password.

Enabling the comment feature

If your end user has Acrobat Professional, he or she can add comments right away. But not every client owns a copy of Acrobat Professional; they may only have Adobe Reader, which does not allow commenting by default. So if you want direct feedback added to the wireframe, you will need to enable the feature within Acrobat Professional.

1 Type your password at the password window.

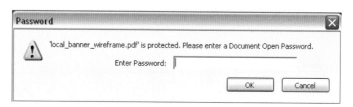

The wireframe opens in Acrobat.

2 Select Comments > Enable For Commenting And Analysis In Adobe Reader.

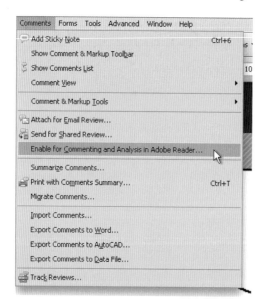

Acrobat prompts you to save the file immediately. Feel free to overwrite the existing file.

And that's it. Yes, we did something in fewer than five steps!

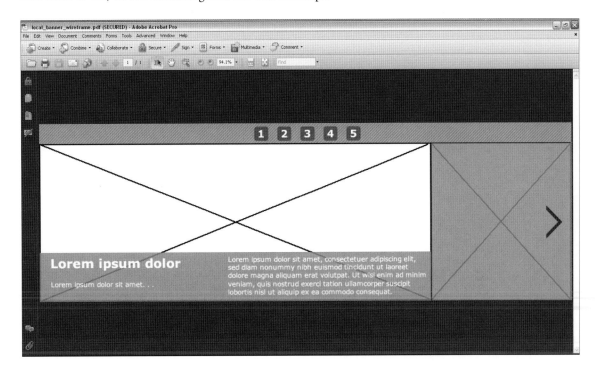

Review questions

1 What are the benefits of using a master page?

2 What are the steps for sharing a layer to other pages?

3 How do you create a copy of an existing page?

4 What is the purpose of a wireframe?

5 How can symbols help you when building a wireframe?

Review answers

1 The master page can be used for displaying common elements across all pages in a design, such as a header or a background. This speeds up the creation of other pages, because all pages are initially based on the master page. When you edit an object on a master page, that edit is reflected on all pages in the design.

2 Select the layer you wish to share from the Layers panel, and choose Share Layer To Pages from the Layers panel menu. In the Share Layer To Pages dialog box, add the pages you wish to share the layer with, and click OK.

3 To create a copy of an existing page, drag the page from the Pages panel to the Add/Duplicate Page icon at the bottom of the Pages panel.

4 A wireframe is a simplistic rendition of the final project. The idea behind a wireframe is that it can be quickly built and just as easily discarded when it has served its purpose. The goal of a wireframe is to describe an application's function, flow, and general layout, without focusing on the aesthetics of the final project.

5 Using symbols when building a wireframe speeds up your work. There is no need to create new shapes on other pages for the same intended purpose, and no need to even copy and paste. With symbols, you just drag and drop them on to the canvas, and if they are vector objects, scale as needed to fit your requirements.

11

ADVANCED PROTOTYPING

Lesson overview

In Fireworks, you can create complex, interactive prototypes to demonstrate how a final project will work. As you work through this lesson, remember that Fireworks is an excellent graphics editor—but keep in mind that it is not designed to be, nor should you expect it to be, an HTML web-page editor.

For the purposes of prototyping, you won't be focusing on image optimization to any great degree in the lesson, and you'll only use slices when they are needed for visual effects such as rollovers.

In this lesson, you'll learn how to do the following:

- Create a multipage website prototype
- Use the Slice tool for interactivity
- Use the Hotspot tool to trigger a disjointed rollover (a pop-up window)
- Simulate a Spry data table (disjointed rollovers)
- Preview an interactive web-page design in a web browser
- Export an interactive mockup of a website

 This lesson will take about 2 hours to complete. Copy the Lesson11 folder into the Lessons folder that you created on your hard drive for these projects (or create it now, if you haven't already done so). As you work on this lesson, you won't preserve the start files. If you need to restore the start files, copy them from the *Adobe Fireworks CS5 Classroom in a Book* CD.

Fireworks gives you the power to create a realistic, fully interactive, clickable HTML mockup using standard Fireworks tools. Creating button rollovers and emulating pop-up windows is a snap.

Prototype orientation

Many of the concepts you learned in Lesson 10 apply to this lesson as well, so you'll have the opportunity to practice them again.

You'll open the completed website prototype first (check_mag_site_final.fw.png), in order to familiarize yourself with the final goals. If you are prompted about missing fonts, simply choose Maintain Appearance for now, as we will not be interacting with this file much. This is the completed web-page mockup that you will be building during this lesson.

You may recall from the last lesson that we moved the Pages panel into its own group in the panel dock—a setup we find more useful and convenient than its default location. If your Pages panel is not still in its own group, drag to position it as such now.

Master page

In Lesson 10, you learned that the Master page is an optional item. Use it if you have visual elements that will be common to all pages and in the same physical location. In this sample file, you have common elements for the header, so it uses a Master page.

1 Open the check_mag_site_final.fw.png file.

2 Select the Master page at the top of the Pages panel. Several graphics that are common to each page in the mockup are present in the Master page.

3 Click Show Slices And Hotspots in the Tools panel.

There are several hotspots and slices applied to the objects on the Master page. The links are common to each page, so it makes sense to apply the Web objects to the Master page. Creating button symbols for the navigation generated the slices. Button symbols were chosen for the navigation in order to create rollover effects.

4 Open the Web layer.

The hotspots appear in the Web layer, but because the slices for the main navigation are part of the button symbols, you won't see them in the Web layer. You will only see the slices by double-clicking on a button symbol.

Content pages

In this final mockup, all the pages have been named using standard naming conventions. This is especially important because you will be generating HTML pages from this file. You will look now at a page that includes the Master page elements as well as its own distinct graphics.

1 Select the page called index. You may recall this page from Lesson 8 ("Optimizing for the Web").

2   Zoom out enough that you can see most of the document.

3   Click Show Slices And Hotspots in the Tools panel.

The hotspots from the Master page are visible, but there are no slices for the graphics on the page itself. Because this is a prototype only, slices are kept to a minimum and used only when visual effects are needed. Once the prototype is approved, the designer can come back to slice up the graphics for optimization and export for the final web pages.

Note also that you cannot select the slices or hotspots that are located on the Master page.

Note: As a prototype, PNG 24 could also have been used as the default optimization setting, but the resulting files would be significantly larger and might create a noticeable lag when the pages are viewed online for testing.

4   Click off the canvas to make sure no objects are selected, and open the Optimize panel.

The base optimization setting for this (and for all the other pages in this design for that matter) is set to JPEG – Higher Quality. Overall, this is a good choice for image quality.

5   Switch to the feature page. This page does make use of slices, but only for rollover effects and links to subpages of the features page.

6   Turn off slices and hotspots, and then click the Preview button at the top of the document window.

7   Select the Pointer tool and move your mouse over the thumbnail photos on the left side of the page. Note the subtle rollover effect.

8   Close the file without saving it.

Fleshing out the prototype

To expedite the lesson, most of the art for the pages has already been added. You will, however, create the Master page and two new pages, as well as add the art to the new pages. Much of your time will be spent building the interactivity for this prototype.

Creating the Master page

Because this is a website mockup and pages may vary in length, only common elements that appear at the top of the page will be included in the Master page.

1   Open check_mag_site_start.fw.png. If you are prompted about missing fonts, choose Replace Fonts and select fonts on your system that look similar to any fonts you're missing. If you don't know what a missing font looks like, search the Internet for samples.

2   Select the header page, if it is not already active.

3   Select the index page. The header content is missing for the index page and all subsequent pages.

4 Right-click (Windows) or Control-click (Mac) on the header page in the Pages panel, and choose Set As Master Page.

5 Rename the Master page to **common.**

6 Select the index page and note that the header area is now visible.

7 Save the file.

Adding more pages

Next you will add more pages to the mockup:

1 Select the page called blog.

2 Click the Add/Duplicate Page icon and rename the new page to **video.**

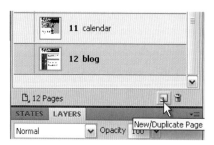

3 Select the new page, and then repeat Step 2, this time naming the page **fashion**.

You will be adding content to these pages shortly, but first you will add the main navigation.

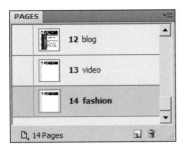

Note: Page names become HTML filenames when you export as HTML And Images or CSS And Images, so it's a good idea to follow standard naming conventions for page names, just as you would with slice names. Avoid spaces and special characters, and to keep things really simple, only use lowercase letters.

Creating rollover navigation

To show the client the intended rollover effect for the navigation bar, each piece of text should be linked to a button symbol. This is the most expeditious option, as it allows you to set up rollover effects and customize the text label for each instance in the navigation. If you don't wish to show a rollover effect, you could use hotspots instead of button symbols.

1 Select the Master page.

2 In the Layers panel, expand the HEADER 1 layer.

3 On the Canvas, zoom in to 200%.

4 On the canvas, right-click or Control-click on the text block FEATURES to bring up the context menu.

5 Choose Convert To Symbol.

6 When the Create Symbol dialog box appears, name the symbol **navigation** and choose Button as the type; then click OK.

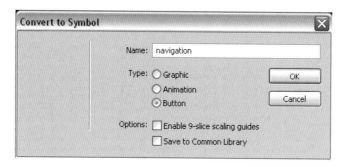

● **Note:** It may look like the symbol is being added to the ADS sublayer, but if you look closely at the Layers panel, you will see that the ADS sublayer is collapsed.

7 In the Properties panel, change the button name to features.

8 In the Optimize panel, change the Export file format to PNG 8. You can use the default settings for this format.

9 Hold down the Option or Alt key and press the right arrow key four times. There are now five instances for your navigation.

10 In the HEADER 1 layer of the Layers panel, select the topmost button symbol, hold down the Shift key, and select the bottom button symbol. All five copies should be selected.

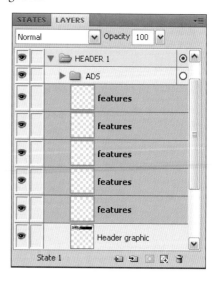

11 Open the Align panel and type a value of **50** in the Space field.

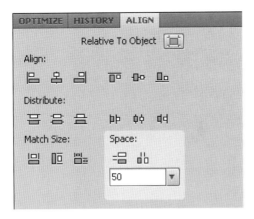

12 Click the Space Evenly Horizontally icon to distribute the navigation buttons.

13 Make sure that the Show Slices And Hotspots icon is selected and that you can see the green slice boxes around the text.

14 Select the second button and in the Properties inspector, change the Text label to **FASHION**.

15 Change the Button name to **fashion**.

16 Change the text labels and button names for the other buttons to:

CALENDAR

VIDEO

BLOG

For consistency, keep the button names in lowercase lettering.

Now that the text lengths have changed, you need to adjust the spacing between each button.

17 Select all five buttons.

18 In the Align panel, make sure the Space value is still set to 50 and click the Space Evenly Horizontally icon again.

▶ **Tip:** If you can't see your slices, and the Show Slices And Hotspots tool has been selected, try clicking Hide Slices And Hotspots, then reselecting the Show tool. You can toggle between the two settings by pressing 2 on your keyboard.

Adding the rollover effect

We have the initial (or Up) state of our buttons, but we need to create the rollover state. With button symbols, this is very easy.

1 Double-click any of the buttons. Everything else on the canvas fades slightly as you're now in the Edit-in-Place mode for the symbol.

2 In the Properties panel, change to the Over state.

3 Click the Copy Up Graphic button.

4 Select the text with the Pointer tool.

5 In the Properties panel, change the color of the text to **#0099FF**.

6 Double-click on the canvas, away from the button, to exit the Edit-in-Place mode.

By editing the button symbol, you ensure that all the buttons receive the same rollover effect.

Adding hyperlinks

With the buttons in place, you need to make them interactive. Each button needs to point to a specific page in the design.

1 Select the FEATURES button.

2 In the Properties panel, choose feature.htm from the bottom section of the Link list.

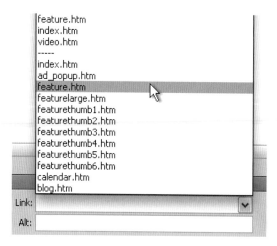

3 In the Alt field, type **Visit the features page**.

4 Link the other buttons to the following pages:

- FASHION: fashion.htm
- CALENDAR: calendar.htm
- VIDEO: video.htm
- BLOG: blog.htm

5 Add suitable text to the Alt field for these buttons as well.

6 Save the file.

There are other areas we wish to serve as navigation, also. You will now add hotspots to a couple of the graphics.

7 Right-click on the watch image and choose Insert Hotspot from the context menu.

8 In the Properties panel, set the link for this hotspot to ad_popup.htm.

9 In the Alt field, type **View the watch advertisement**.

10 Select the rectangular hotspot tool from the tools panel and draw a hotspot over most of the website name. The final dimensions should be 389 pixels x 100 pixels.

11 Set the position of the hotspot to X: 71 pixels and Y: 97 pixels.

12 In the Alt field, type **Return to home page**.

13 Set the link for this hotspot to index.htm.

You should now have two hotspots and five slices on the Master page, all linked and ready to go.

14 Save the file.

Customizing page dimensions

The index page was based on the original page dimensions, but if you scroll down to the bottom of the page, you'll see a lot of empty space between the text and the footer. This white space is unnecessary, so you will shorten the length of this specific page so the footer is closer to the text.

1 Select the index page in the Pages panel.

2 Right-click (or Control-click) on the footer layer in the Layers panel.

3 Choose Detach Shared Layer. This retains a copy of the footer on the current page, but it is no longer linked to the original shared layer. You need to do this in order to customize the position of the footer text on this specific page. If you left the layer as a shared layer, you would be altering the position of the footer on all the pages that share the layer.

4 Select the footer text using the Pointer tool.

5 In the Properties panel, change the Y value to 940.

6 Choose Modify > Canvas > Canvas Size.

7 Set the height to 970 pixels.

8 Change the anchor point to the top middle button.

9 Select the Current Page Only option, and then click OK.

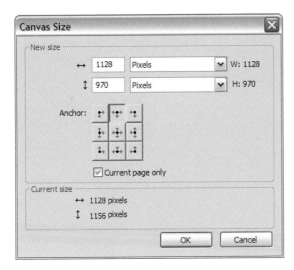

Image rollover effects

The feature page is where you really start to work! Each thumbnail on the left side needs to have a rollover effect applied to it, and also needs interactivity to link to a different mockup page. You'll create a rollover effect that changes the thumbnails from a sepia-tone image to a full-color image. You will be working with commands, states, slices, and shared layers for this part of the exercise. Hey, we did say this was the advanced lesson, after all!

Adding a rollover state

A rollover effect needs content on a separate state for the rollover to work. You will add the new state in this exercise. Because the content of each thumbnail is different, you can't use button symbols to speed things up. So you will be building these rollovers by hand.

1 Select the feature page.

2 In the Layers panel, expand the feature layer.

This layer holds all the objects that are specific to the feature pages. To further structure the file, many objects have been placed in separate sublayers. This feature layer has also been shared to other pages, as indicated by the familiar icon at the right of the layer name.

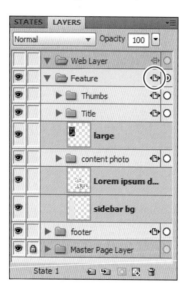

3   In the Layers panel options, choose Share Layer To Pages.

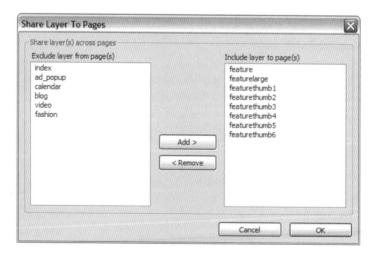

The Share Layer To Pages dialog box shows that this layer is shared to a total of eight pages. As you learned in the previous lesson, this sharing can expedite some editing tasks; as you change objects in a shared layer, those changes are propagated to all the pages that share the layer. This includes the editing, visibility, and addition/deletion of objects or sublayers within the shared layer.

The importance—and limitations—of sublayers

Sublayers are a great organizational tool; rather than having to search for individual objects within a long list of layers, you can group related objects into sublayers.

Layer and sublayer hierarchy is also preserved as layer groups when you save a page as a Photoshop file. Similarly, if you open a Photoshop file in Fireworks that contains Photoshop layer groups, that layer hierarchy would also be preserved.

Sublayers do have their limitations, however. When you copy a layer that contains sublayers, only the parent layer elements are copied to the clipboard; sublayers are ignored.

If you copy a sublayer, only the objects within the sublayer are copied. So if you were to paste the clipboard contents into a new design, only the objects—and not the actual sublayer that contained them—would be pasted.

If you share a layer to other pages, all sublayers are automatically shared with that page as well. You cannot selectively share certain sublayers with different pages.

4 Click Cancel to dismiss the Share Layer To Pages dialog box.

5 Expand the thumbs sublayer, and select the thumb1 object in the sublayer.

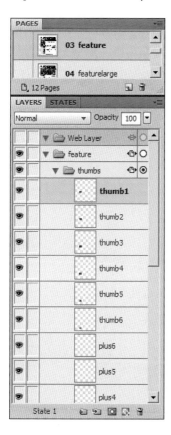

6 Scroll down in the Layers panel until you see the thumb6 object.

7 Hold down Shift, and click on the thumb6 object. This selects all six thumbnail images.

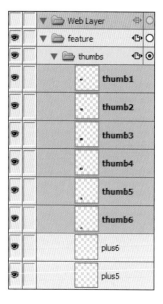

8 Choose Edit > Copy.

9 Open the States panel.

All files opened in Fireworks have at least one state—the current one. You will now add another state to the feature page.

10 Choose Add States from the States panel menu.

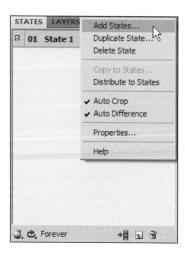

11 When the Add States dialog box appears, click OK. The defaults are fine for our simple purposes.

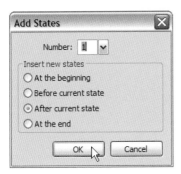

A new empty state appears in the States panel.

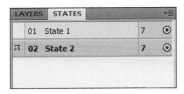

12 Go back to the Layers panel, and make sure the feature layer is still active.

13 Choose Edit > Paste. The color thumbnails appear on the new state, in exactly the same location as on the original state.

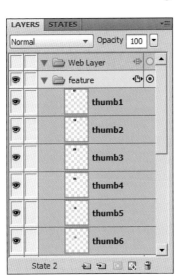

▶ **Tip:** You can also drag the selected images to the thumbs sublayer in the Layers panel.

In order for the rollover to work in the mockup, the new state needs to be added to all pages.

14 Select the featurelarge page.

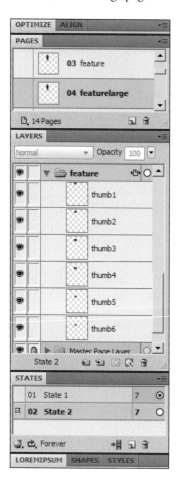

15 Click the New/Duplicate state button in the States panel.

The new state appears, containing your rollover images. In this figure, we have separated the States panel from the Layers panel, so you can more easily see the relationship between the panels.

16 Repeat steps 15 and 16 for the six remaining feature pages.

Creating the rollover effect

You will make a small change to the State 1 thumbnails so that you can establish the rollover effect.

1 In any feature page where you can easily select all six thumbnails, select State 1 again. This is a shared layer, remember, so we can edit it from any page that it's shared to.

Note: If you were building this prototype from the start, you would probably add the rollover effect to the first page you create, saving you the time of going back and adding in the rollover graphics to every completed page.

2 Shift-click to select each thumbnail, if they are not already selected.

3 Choose Commands > Creative > Convert To Sepia Tone.

This applies an editable Live Filter to all six images.

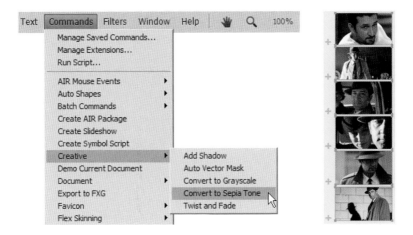

Creating the rollover slices

Now you will add the slices needed for the rollovers. Make sure all six objects are still selected.

1 Right-click or Control-click on any of the six thumbnails, and choose Insert Rectangular Slice from the context menu.

Note: If for some reason the context menu does not give you this option, first check to make sure all the images are selected, and then choose Edit > Insert > Rectangular Slice.

2 Choose Multiple from the alert box. You need multiple individual slices, instead of one large slice covering all six images, so that each image can have an independent rollover effect applied to its slice.

Each thumbnail now has a slice applied to it, and the slices are currently selected.

3 Choose JPEG – Better Quality from the Slice Export Settings in the Properties panel. Even though we're not too worried about optimization settings, JPEG will render the thumbnails best in the clickable prototype.

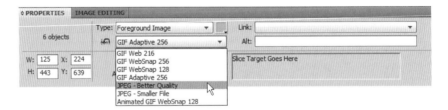

Because these rollover effects are going to be used on many pages, you should share the slices.

4 Right-click or Control-click on the Web layer in the Layers panel, and choose New Sub Layer from the context menu.

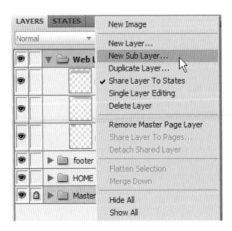

5 Change the sublayer name to **thumbs**, and click OK.

6 The slices you created should still be selected. If they are not, select the top slice in the Web layer, and then hold Shift and click the bottom slice.

7 Drag the six slices to the thumbs web sublayer.

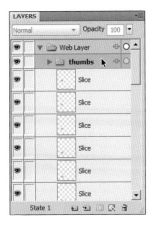

8 Choose Share Layer To Pages from the Layers panel options.

9 Add all the feature pages to the Include Layer To Page(s) list, and then click OK.

▶ **Tip:** If you are finding it difficult to drag the objects to the correct layer, you can choose Edit > Cut, select the thumbs web sublayer, and choose Edit > Paste.

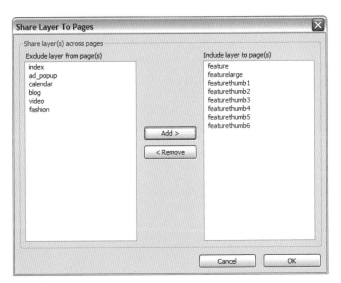

▶ **Tip:** It can be difficult to tell when objects are part of any sublayer. When in doubt, collapse the sublayer. If the objects become hidden, you know they are part of that sublayer.

Naming your slices

Even though you are building a mockup here, it is entirely likely that these thumbnails—and their rollover counterparts—will be needed for the final website. With that in mind, you will name each slice.

Note: If the active slice on the canvas is not the topmost thumbnail image (which can happen, depending on the order in which the slices were added), name it accordingly. For example, if the slice is the third from the top, name it thumb3.

1   In the new thumbs web sublayer, select the top slice in the stack. Then, locate the active slice object on the canvas, which should be the slice that appears superimposed on the topmost thumbnail image.

2   In the thumbs web sublayer, name this slice **thumb1**. A generic, functional name is a good idea, in case the image content changes.

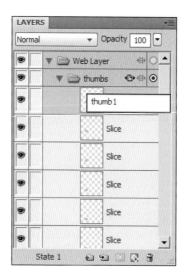

Note: Because slices are usually exported, each slice name must be unique, or you run the risk of overwriting your graphics while you export them.

3   Select each of the remaining thumbnail slices, one at a time, and rename them, from top to bottom, **thumb2**, **thumb3**, **thumb4**, **thumb5**, and **thumb6**.

4   When the naming is done, save your work.

▶ **Tip:** If your slice or object names have a common element (such as thumb, in this case), save yourself some typing by selecting the text while your cursor is active in the object's label field, and then copying it. When you double-click on the next object you need to name, just paste the copied text into the field and finish off the name.

Adding rollover behaviors

Now it's time to add interactivity to these slices. But first, let's recap. You have two states for the thumbnails, each containing a different version of each thumbnail image. The feature layer is shared to all the feature pages. There is a uniquely named image slice covering each thumbnail. These slices are in a web sublayer called thumbs, and that web sublayer is shared to all the feature pages as well. Get ready to make all this work—states, thumbnail versions, slices, shared layers—come together as rollovers.

1   Make sure all six slices are selected. You will see a small circle in the middle of each slice. This is the *behavior handle*.

2   Click on the behavior handle of any of the six slices.

3   Choose Add Simple Rollover Behavior. This adds a basic swap image behavior to each of the selected slices.

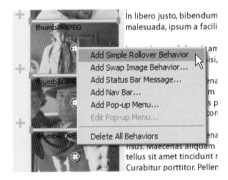

What are behaviors?

Behaviors are a quick way to add JavaScript functionality to a web-page mockup, without having to write a single line of JavaScript code. Image rollovers are a pretty common use of JavaScript in web pages (although CSS-based rollover effects are becoming more popular). Behaviors are also used in Dreamweaver for creating rollover effects, navigation bar effects, and many other JavaScript-driven events.

4 Save the file.

5 Choose File > Preview In Browser > Preview In [default browser]. In our case, the default browser is Firefox. Yours may very well be a different web browser.

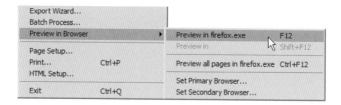

When the web browser loads the mockup, move your mouse over the thumbnails. Each image should change from a sepia-tone to a full-color image.

6 Close the browser, and return to Fireworks.

Emulating pop-up windows

Each of the large images in our design is a unique size, and the goal for the prototype is to display each image as if it were popping up on top of the feature page. Having a unique slice for each different image and attempting to achieve this effect on a single page in Fireworks would be problematic, because Fireworks handles overlapping slices by generating multiple smaller slices to make up the image. The result is a lot of small images on export, with the potential for unpredictable display results.

In order to mimic a pop-up window, where the window varies in size, you can use pages to display the unique content.

The problem with overlapping slices

Overlapping slices can cause unexpected results, because Fireworks must decide how to cut up the imagery beneath those slices. If a file is exported as HTML And Images, the result can be a series of smaller slices. For example, two overlapping slices may result in three or more images, just to re-create the overlapped effect. For prototypes this is not a big deal because the goal of a prototype is to provide a realistic mechanism for user interaction and feedback, but you still end up with a lot of small graphics, which can be problematic if you are trying to locate a specific file.

The CSS And Images export won't allow you to overlap slices and still produce a standards-based page. If Fireworks detects overlapping slices during this type of export, you are warned about the problem, and Fireworks exports the file as an absolutely positioned web page.

If you export overlapping slices manually (right-click on a slice and choose Export Selected Slice), the topmost overlapping slice is the only one that is exported correctly. Slices that are lower in the stacking order of the web layer are literally cut at the point where the slices intersect.

For example, if you have a logo on a background image and need to export both as separate individual images, you have to export one object at a time while hiding the other object (and changing the stacking order in the Layers panel).

Now many web-page designs have overlapping elements. How do you resolve this issue when you need to export graphics for the real web page? A common workflow solution is to create an "assets" page that contains any artwork that would be overlapping within the design. Each object and its slice are kept clear of other objects. The objects can then be exported from this assets page.

You must now add links to these six thumbnail slices.

1   Select each slice, and choose the appropriate link from the Properties panel Link menu. For example, the thumb1 slice should link to featurethumb1.htm.

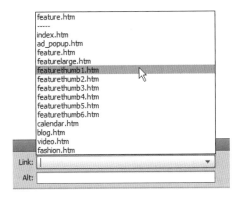

Note: While inline images in web pages require alternate text, we're not requiring you to fill in this image description in this exercise, because this is only a prototype and not the final website.

You should also add a link for the main feature image, though you won't bother with a rollover for this one.

2 Draw a hotspot over the large plus sign (+) and the word ENLARGE.

3 Set the link for this hotspot to go to featurelarge.htm.

4 Make sure the hotspot is in the thumbs web sublayer. Drag it into the sublayer, if necessary.

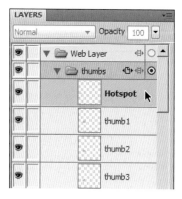

Are pop-up windows evil?

The dreaded pop-up window: it's so feared that all major browsers have some form of defense against allowing it to display without the user's permission. These "pop-up blocker" mechanisms are in place because, too often, pop-up windows are either used incorrectly—windows popping up all over the desktop because they were not set up properly—or used as an intentional annoyance by some nefarious advertiser, bent on dominating the user's desktop with a myriad of ads.

But while many users consider them irritating, pop-up windows, when properly executed, can be useful for a website. There are many things to consider when creating true pop-up windows, in order to make them accessible and searchable (two things that contribute to their usefulness). It's beyond the scope of this book to discuss those details, but you can check out sitepoint.com for a discussion on building better JavaScript pop-up windows (www.sitepoint.com/article/perfect-pop-up).

5 Rename this latest hotspot to **main_feature**.

6 When you have added all the links, save the file.

7 Choose File > Preview In Browser > Preview All Pages In [default browser], and test the links.

Clicking on the thumbnails should take you to the proper page.

Emulating a Spry data table

Ajax (Asynchronous JavaScript and XML) gives you the ability to create dynamic web pages without forcing the entire web page to refresh. Spry, Adobe's framework for Ajax, is geared to making it easier for designers to create these dynamic elements within Dreamweaver. Granted, these definitions are very simplistic—a detailed discussion of either Spry or Ajax is not within the scope of this book—but with a little understanding of the desired end result, you can, for example, mock up the feature page like a dynamic photo gallery or data table within Fireworks. Our sample Check website requires the creation of a dynamic data area for the calendar page, and Fireworks—with your help—can create the look and feel for client feedback, before a single line of code is written.

1 Select the calendar page.

2 Open the States panel.

The calendar page has a total of seven states, each one representing a different state for the calendar menu or the detail section of the data table.

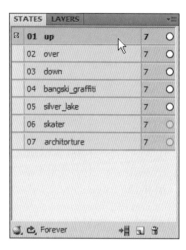

3 Click on the silver_lake state, and note how the left side of the page is updated with new content. (We've undocked the States panel so you can better see the relationship.)

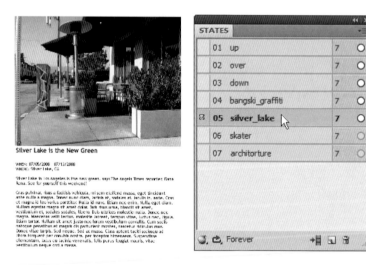

4 Switch to the Layers panel. Here you can select different states by choosing from the Current State pop-up menu at the lower left of the panel.

5 Choose the up state. Note the orange-colored background behind the calendar menu.

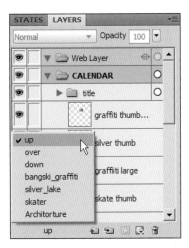

6 Choose the over state, and note the change in the background color.

By adding in some new content, and making use of slices and behaviors, you will make this into a completely interactive page.

7 Select the up state again.

8 While holding down the Shift key, use the Pointer tool to click on the large black and white photo and the text block on the left side of the page.

9 Right-click or Control-click, and choose Insert Rectangular Slice.

10 Because you have more than one object selected, a dialog box appears, asking if you want to create single or multiple slices. Click the Single button, so that one slice covers both objects. Change the Slice export settings in the Properties panel to JPEG – Better Quality.

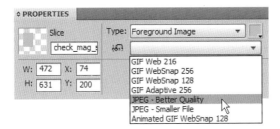

11 Rename the slice **table_data**.

12 Change the height of the slice to 680 pixels.

13 Move over to the calendar section on the right of the page, and with the Zoom tool, draw a box over the top thumbnail and text in the calendar. You want to be able to see the background from side to side.

14 Select the Slice tool, and draw a slice that covers the orange background, thumbnail, and text for the top event. The slice should include a bit of orange background at the bottom.

15 Select the Pointer tool, hold down the Alt (Windows) or Option (Mac) key, and drag copies of the slice object over the other three calendar events. Position the slices with the help of the smart guides.

16 You'll see that the Skate event requires a larger slice than you've created, so drag the control points of the slice to set a dimension that covers the entire area. When you're done, there should be no gaps between the slices.

17 Select all four slices.

18 If necessary, change the Slice export settings in the Properties panel to JPEG – Better Quality.

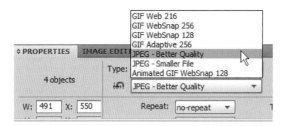

19 In the Properties panel, rename the four slices, from the top to the bottom, **cal_event1**, **cal_event2**, **cal_event3**, and **cal_event4**.

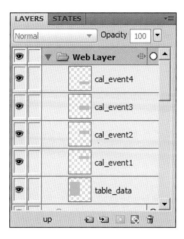

Adding content to empty states

A couple states in the calendar page need content added to them for the rollover magic to work.

1 In the Layers panel, select the calendar layer from the Layers panel, and then choose the skater state from the Current State drop-down menu at the bottom right of the Layers panel.

2 Choose File > Import, and browse to the Lesson11 folder.

3 Locate and open the skater.fw.png file. Make sure the Insert After Current Page option is not selected.

4 When the import icon appears, place it at the upper-left corner of the table_data slice.

Note: If the imported images do not appear exactly where you expect, use the arrow keys to accurately reposition the visible parts of the objects so they are covered by the slice.

5   Click to import the file.

6   Select the architorture state, and repeat steps 1–4, importing the architorture. fw.png file this time.

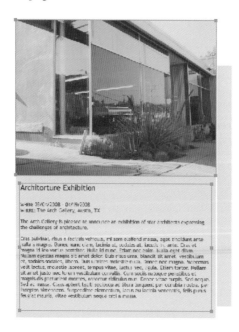

7   Save your work.

Working with behaviors

Creating this simulation is fun, and probably a lot easier than you think. You will be adding prebuilt JavaScript behaviors and then editing them with the Behaviors panel.

Adding the behaviors

Adding behaviors in Fireworks is very easy, as you are about to see.

1 Still in the Layers panel, select the up state.

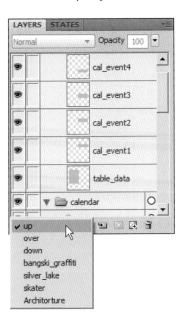

2 Use the Pointer tool to select the cal_event1 slice.

3 Click the Behavior handle and choose Add Nav Bar.

The Set Nav Bar Image dialog box gives you the chance to set other optional settings, but you will leave those options deselected.

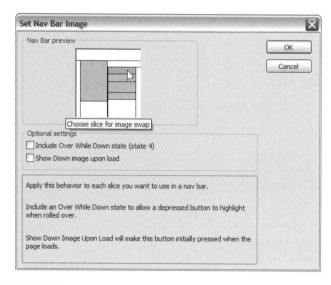

4 Click OK.

5 Use the Pointer tool to drag the behavior handle over to the table_data slice. A curved blue line will connect the slices, and a dialog box will appear.

6 Select bangski_graffiti (4) from the Swap Image From menu. This creates your remote image change.

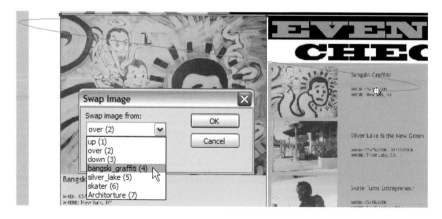

7 Click the More Options button.

8 Deselect the Restore Image OnMouseOut option. This makes the effect "sticky," meaning it won't change back unless there is additional user interaction.

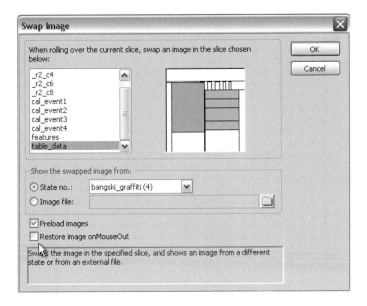

9 Click OK.

10 Repeat this process with the other event slices; be sure to select the right rollover for each—associating the cal_event2 slice with silver_lake (5), and so on.

Editing JavaScript behaviors

You have just created in a visual manner a series of JavaScript events. As mentioned earlier, Fireworks (and Dreamweaver) call these prebuilt events *behaviors*. Using them does not require any knowledge of JavaScript, nor do you need to edit the actual JavaScript code. However, you can customize the behaviors using the Behaviors panel.

The default event for this type of image swap is for the table_data image to change when the user's mouse moves over event slices. This is referred to as a remote, or disjointed, rollover. In your case, though, you want the appropriate table_data image to swap in when the user clicks on the matching slice, rather than when the user hovers the mouse over the area.

This is where the Behaviors panel comes to your aid.

1 Select the cal_event1 slice.

2 Choose Window > Behaviors.

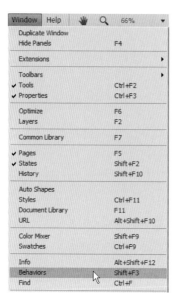

3 Select the OnMouseOver event, which is part of the Swap Image action.

4 Choose OnClick, the second item in the list.

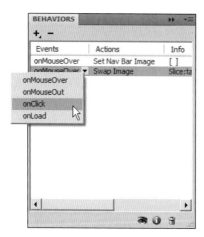

5 Select the cal_event2 slice on the canvas.

6 In the Behaviors panel, select the OnMouseOver event, which is part of the Swap Image action.

7 Choose OnClick.

8 Repeat the process with the other two slices, and save your work.

▶ **Tip:** If the Behaviors panel is getting in the way, you can either collapse it by clicking the Behaviors tab, or you can dock it with the other panel groups on the right side of the application.

Previewing the remote rollover

You will now preview the rollover effect right in the main workspace.

1 To test out our dynamic data table simulation, click the Preview button at the top of the document window.

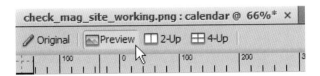

2 In the Tools panel, choose Hide Slices And Hotspots.

3 Move your mouse over the top slice. The background gets lighter. That is your swap image at work.

4 Move down to the next slice.

The silver lake event button gets brighter, and the graffiti button goes back to normal. As you move from event to event, the swapped image is restored. This is the standard mouseover behavior people expect to see.

5 Click on the silver lake event.

The left side of the page updates with the silver_lake state, and the event remains highlighted. This information will remain until you click on another event.

6 Click on the skater event. Again, the left side updates.

7 Switch back to the Original view, and save the file.

Completing the prototype

You have accomplished quite a bit so far—just a little more work to do before this prototype is complete.

Populating the last pages

Remember near the beginning of this lesson you added two new pages—video and fashion. Well, your crowning touches on this prototype are to add the visuals for those pages.

1 Select the video page.

2 Drag a vertical guide, and place it 71 pixels in from the left. Remember, to add guides, the rulers must be visible. If Tooltips are visible (View > Tooltips), they will help you with placing the guides accurately.

3 Drag down a horizontal guide and place it at 200 pixels.

These guides will help you import the content for the video page.

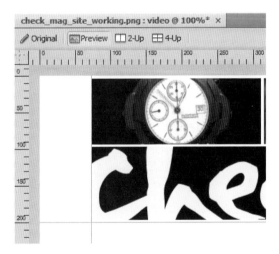

4 Choose File > Import, and browse to the Lesson11 folder.

5 Locate and open the new_pages.fw.png file.

6 Navigate to the video page and choose Import from the Preview window. Again, make sure that Insert After Current Page is not selected.

7 Place the import cursor at the intersection of the two guides, and click to import.

The video content is now in place.

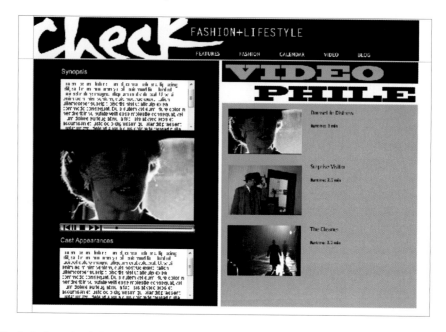

8 Switch to the fashion page, and set up guides at the same positions.

9 Import the fashion page from the new_pages.fw.png file.

10 Place your import cursor at the intersection of the two guides, and click to import.

Adding the footer

A few last steps remain to complete the prototype; you need to add the footer to the new pages.

1 Select the index page and, using the Pointer tool, select the footer text object on the canvas.

2 Copy the object and go back to the fashion page.

3 Select the empty Layer 1 in the Layers panel and then paste the text.

4 Rename the layer to footer.

5 In the Properties panel, set the Y value for the text to 1150 pixels.

6 Select Modify > Canvas > Canvas Size.

7 Set the canvas height to 1200 pixels and choose the top-center anchor point button. Make sure that Current Page Only is selected.

8 Select the empty Layer 1 in the video page, and paste the text again.

9 Position the text at 830 pixels.

10 Select Modify > Canvas > Canvas Size and change the height to 880 pixels. Remember to center the anchor point and make sure that Current Page Only is selected.

11 Save your work.

Exporting the prototype

Your final step in the prototype is to export the design so the client can test-drive the flow and function of the site (and of course, be impressed with your graphic design skills!).

1 In the Pages panel, select all the pages except the Master page.

2 Choose File > Export.

3 Browse to the Lesson11 folder, and create a new folder there called **check_site**.

4 Open (Windows) or select (Mac) the new folder.

● **Note:** The HTML And Images option generates a series of table-based HTML pages, which are fine for prototype testing. However, due to the vast number of images and the rigid table structure of the pages, this export is not recommended for use as the final production website.

5 Choose HTML And Images from the Export list.

6 Make sure that the HTML field reads Export HTML File and that the Slices field reads Export Slices.

7 Choose Selected Pages from the Pages list.

8 Make sure Include Areas Without Slices is selected. You sliced only a specific number of elements—mostly for interactivity purposes—and if you don't export unsliced areas, your web pages will not look right.

9 Make sure Put Images In Subfolder is selected, too, just to keep things a bit more orderly. You can browse to an images folder in your prototype directory, or let Fireworks create a default images folder for you.

10 Click the Options button and select the Table tab.

11 Choose Nested Tables, No Spacers from the Space With menu. This reduces the table complexity a little, but is by no means mandatory for the export.

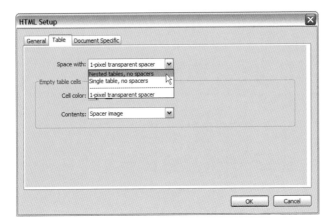

12 Select the Document Specific tab.

13 In the State Names section, make sure the naming convention is set to State # (f2, f3, f4…).

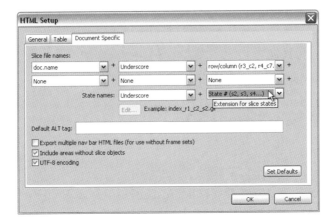

14 Click OK to close the HTML setup dialog box, and then click Save (Windows) or Export (Mac) to complete the export process.

There is no progress bar for this export process, but you should see the hour-glass in Windows or the spinning beach ball on the Mac. The export process for this design should be finished within a minute or two.

15 Using Windows Explorer or the Mac Finder, locate your prototype folder.

You will see 14 web pages and a folder called images.

16 Open the images folder and you will see a frightening number of graphics. As discussed in earlier lessons, Fireworks exports everything as graphics when you choose the Export HTML And Images option. Any areas that were not manually sliced are exported using the Fireworks autonaming and autoslicing process.

Again, as this is for prototyping only, it is not something you should be overly concerned about. It's also a good example of why you should not use the HTML And Images export to generate final website pages.

You're done! Feel free to double-click on the index page to launch your mockup in a web browser, and test out the links and other interactive elements.

Review questions

1 What is a "remote" rollover?

2 How do you add new states to a page?

3 What are behaviors, and how do you apply them?

4 How do you edit JavaScript behaviors?

5 How do you turn a completed multipage Fireworks design into a clickable Web prototype?

Review answers

1 When you click or mouse over an area on a web page, a visual change occurs in a different location on the same page. The effect is called a remote rollover. You can create this effect in Fireworks using a combination of hotspots and slices, or slices alone, along with Fireworks behaviors to add in the necessary JavaScript.

2 You add new states by choosing New State from the States panel menu.

3 Behaviors are prebuilt JavaScript functions that can be added by clicking the behavior handle of either a hotspot or image slice object.

4 You can edit applied behaviors by opening the Behaviors panel (Window > Behaviors). Select the slice or hotspot that has the attached behaviors, and then select the specific behavior in the Behaviors panel. You can also add additional behaviors using the Behaviors panel.

5 Choose File > Export, browse to the desired directory, choose HTML And Images from the Export menu, and make sure that Include Areas Without Slices is selected and that Current Page Only is *not* selected.

INDEX

Entries for bonus supplemental chapters 12 and 13 are noted with the letter S.

drawing vector shapes, 7–8, 80
Dreamweaver CS5, S:88–S:99
    copying and pasting to, S:88–S:92
    creating pods for, S:95–S:99
    round-trip editing using, S:92–S:95
duplicating states, 34

E

edge pixels, 55
Edit Gradient pop-up window, 12, 97, 113
Edit in Place mode, 213
editing
    bitmap masks, 126–127
    button symbols, 220–221
    FXG files, S:85–S:87
    gradients, 113–114
    graphic symbols, 213–215
    JavaScript behaviors, 289–292
    objects within groups, S:9–S:10
    paths, 93
    round-trip, S:92–S:95, S:99
    text, 145–146, 154
    vector masks, 124
Elliptical Marquee tool, 65
e-mail, sending files to, S:26
empty bitmap objects, 58
empty states, 285–286
emulations
    pop-up window, 276–279
    Spry data table, 279–286
Escape key, 41
Expand/Collapse Layer icon, 32
Export Area tool, S:22
Export As Adobe PDF option, 161
Export dialog box, 201, 246–247, S:23
Export FXG And Images option, 161
exporting
    animations, 234
    CSS and Images, 195–203
    files to Photoshop, S:34–S:35
    Flex skins, S:80–S:81
    FXG documents, S:82–S:84
    HTML and Images, 188–195, 296
    optimized files, 170
    overlapping slices, 277
    pages to files, 28
    prototypes, 296–298
    resetting options for, S:24
    saving vs., 161
    specific areas, S:22–S:24
    states, 193–194

wireframes, 246–247
extensions, 13
Eyedropper tool, 113

F

face-lift technique, 58–59
Feathered selection edge, 65
file formats
    Adobe XMP format, S:27
    Fireworks PNG format, 9, 161
    Flash FXG format, S:82
    Photoshop PSD format, 28, S:33–S:34
    for Web graphics, 160–161
file names
    customizing for states, 193
    specifying for symbols, 211
file size
    GIF animations and, 231, 232
    resolution and, 40
    Web optimization and, 160, 169, 177–179
files
    adding metadata to, S:27–S:29
    exporting vs. saving, 161
    saving in Fireworks, 9
Fill Category Pattern submenu, 100
Fill Color box, 97
fills
    gradient, 12–13, 95–97
    vector shape, 7–8
Filmstrip workspace, S:11
filters
    applying to bitmaps, 67
    supported in Flash, S:101
    Unsharp Mask filter, 54–55
    See also Live Filters
Find Source dialog box, S:93, S:108
Fireworks CS5
    AIR functionality in, S:44
    blending modes supported in, S:36
    CSS and, 195–198
    Developer Center, 197, S:81
    Dreamweaver and, S:88–S:99
    Flash and, S:99–S:110
    Flash Catalyst and, S:82
    Illustrator and, S:87
    interface illustration, 5
    native PNG format, 9, 161
    Photoshop and, 28, 119–120, S:30–S:36
    workflow, S:2–S:37
fixed-width text blocks, 143–144

N

naming/renaming
  layers, 30
  objects, 28–29
  slices, 182–183, 274
  states, 34, 193
  symbols, 211
navigation buttons, 220
nested symbols, 228
New Bitmap Image icon, 52, S:65
New Document dialog box, 4, 111
New Flex Skin dialog box, S:75
New From Template dialog box, S:4
New Style dialog box, 133–134
New Sub Layer button, 31
New/Duplicate Layer button, 30
New/Duplicate page icon, 225
No Anti-Alias setting, 149
Numeric Transform options, 51
N-Up feature, 168

O

object-oriented approach, 59
objects
  aligning, 49–50
  determining active, 155
  editing within groups, S:9–S:10
  grouping, 51
  hiding, 43
  layers and, 59
  locking, 33, 43
  naming, 28–29
  overlapping, 198
  placing with guides, 44
  positioning, 43, 49–50, 82–83
  proportions of, 9
  rearranging, 29
  selecting, 64
onion skinning, 228–230
Optimize panel, 161–163
  choosing settings in, 168–169
  view options in, 165, 168
  See also Web optimization
Original view option, 165
Oval Marquee tool, 64
overlapping objects, 198
overlapping slices, 277
Oversampling option, 149

P

page weight, 160, 162
pages, 24, 26–28
  adding, 242–243, 258–259
  content, 255–256
  customizing dimensions of, 264–265
  exporting, 28, S:82–S:84
  importing, 26–27
  master, 240–241, 255, 257–258
  moving between, 27
  reordering, 26, 27
  resetting export options for, S:24
  review question/answer on, 37
  sharing layers to, 266–267
  wireframe, 241–245
Pages panel
  isolating, 239–240
  overview of, 238–240
panels
  accessing, 15
  arranging, 15
  configuring, 13–15
  extensions for, 13
  See also specific panels
paragraph indent, 148
paragraph spacing, 148
password-protected tasks, 247
Path Outline mode, 110
Path panel, 100
Path Scrubbers, 92
paths
  attaching text to, 150–152
  drawing with Pen tool, 91
  fonts converted to, S:45
  methods for editing, 93
  selections converted to, 74–75
  text converted to, S:73
  tools for working with, 92
patterns, applying to vector objects, 100
PDF files, creating interactive, 246–247
Pen tool
  adding points with, 93
  creating custom shapes with, 94–95
  drawing paths with, 91, 151
Pencil bitmap tool, 91
Photoshop
  blending modes supported in, S:36
  customizing export options for, S:34–S:35
  Fireworks integration with, 28, 119–120, S:30–S:36
  importing images from, 118–119

Production Notes

The *Adobe Fireworks CS5 Classroom in a Book* was created electronically using Adobe InDesign CS4. Art was produced using Adobe Fireworks. The Myriad Pro and Warnock Pro OpenType families of typefaces were used throughout this book.

References to company names in the lessons are for demonstration purposes only and are not intended to refer to any actual organization or person.

Images

Photographic images and illustrations are intended for use with the tutorials.

Typefaces used

Adobe Myriad Pro and Adobe Warnock Pro are used throughout the lessons. For more information about OpenType and Adobe fonts, visit www.adobe.com/type/opentype/.

Team credits

The following individuals contributed to the development of this edition of the *Adobe Fireworks CS5 Classroom in a Book*:

Writer: Jim Babbage
Associate Editor: Valerie Witte
Developmental Editor: Brie Gyncild
Production Editor: David Van Ness
Technical Editor: Sheri German
Compositor: WolfsonDesign
Copyeditor: Liz Welch
Proofreader: Patricia Pane
Indexer: James Minkin
Cover design: Eddie Yuen
Interior design: Mimi Heft

Contributor

Jim Babbage Jim Babbage teaches imaging, Web design, and photography in Toronto at Centennial College's Centre for Communication, Media, and Design (centennialcollege.ca/thecentre) and at Humber College's Digital Imaging Training Centre (digital.humber.ca). He is also a creative partner/co-owner of NewMedia Services (newmediaservices.ca), a communications company. Beginning his career as a commercial photographer, Jim started with Photoshop and then moved to Web design, using early versions of Fireworks and Dreamweaver, and was hooked. Jim is a frequent contributor of articles on Fireworks, Dreamweaver, Photoshop, and other general Web topics to the Community MX website (communitymx.com) and adobe.com and has presented at Adobe MAX as well as several other conferences. Jim is also the author of several Fireworks video training titles at Lynda.com, including *Fireworks CS5 Essential Training*.

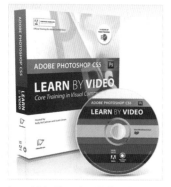

AdobePress

Newly Expanded LEARN BY VIDEO Series

The **Learn by Video** series from video2brain and Adobe Press is the only Adobe-approved video courseware for the Adobe Certified Associate Level certification, and has quickly established itself as one of the most critically-acclaimed training products available on the fundamentals of Adobe software.

Learn by Video offers up to 19 hours of high-quality HD video training presented by experienced trainers, as well as lesson files, assessment quizzes and review materials. The DVD is bundled with a full-color printed book that provides supplemental information as well as a guide to the video topics.

Learn Adobe Photoshop CS5 by Video:
Core Training in Visual Communication
(ISBN 9780321719805)

Up to 19 hours of high-quality video training

Tutorials-to-Go! Transfer selected movies to your iPhone, iPod, or compatible cell phone

Table of Contents never more than a click away

Watch-and-Work mode shrinks the video into a small window while you work in the software

Video player remembers which movie you watched last

Lesson files are included on the DVD

Learn Adobe Flash Professional CS5 by Video:
Core Training in Rich Media Communication
(ISBN 9780321719829)

Additional Titles

- Learn Adobe Photoshop Elements 8 and Adobe Premiere Elements 8 by Video (ISBN 9780321685773)
- Learn Photography Techniques for Adobe Photoshop CS5 by Video (ISBN 9780321734839)
- Learn Adobe After Effects CS5 by Video (ISBN 9780321734860)
- Learn Adobe Flash Catalyst CS5 by Video (ISBN 9780321734853)
- Learn Adobe Illustrator CS5 by Video (ISBN 9780321734815)
- Learn Adobe InDesign CS5 by Video (ISBN 9780321734808)
- Learn Adobe Premiere Pro CS5 by Video (ISBN 9780321734846)

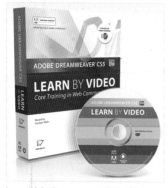

Learn Adobe Dreamweaver CS5 by Video:
Core Training in Web Communication
(ISBN 9780321719812)

For more information go to **www.adobepress.com/learnbyvideo**

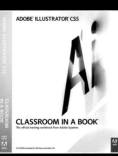

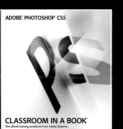

The fastest, easiest, most comprehensive way to learn
Adobe® Creative Suite® 5

Classroom in a Book®, the best-selling series of hands-on software training books, helps you learn the features of Adobe software quickly and easily.

The **Classroom in a Book** series offers what no other book or training program does—an official training series from Adobe Systems, developed with the support of Adobe product experts.

To see a complete list of our Adobe® Creative Suite® 5 titles go to www.peachpit.com/adobecs5

Adobe**Press**

WATCH READ CREATE

Meet Creative Edge.

A new resource of unlimited books, videos and tutorials for creatives from the world's leading experts.

Creative Edge is your one stop for inspiration, answers to technical questions and ways to stay at the top of your game so you can focus on what you do best—being creative.

All for only $24.99 per month for access—any day any time you need it.

creativeedge.com